WEIGHT WATCHERS

INSTANT POT 2018 FREESTYLE

COOKBOOK

100 QUICK, EASY AND HEALTHY WW SMART POINTS RECIPES TO LOSE WEIGHT AND FAT
(LOSE UP TO 30 POUNDS IN 30 DAYS)

By Andrew James

Copyright © Andrew James 2018

All rights reserved. No part of this publication maybe reproduced, stored or transmitted in any form or by any means, electronic, mechanical, photocopying, recording, scanning, or otherwise without written permission from the author. It is illegal to copy this book, post it to a website, or distribute it by any other means without permission.

Andrew James the moral right to be identified as the author of this work.

Table of Contents

CHAPTER ONE 4
   WHAT IS WEIGHT WATCHERS? 4
   BENEFITS OF WEIGHT WATCHERS. 6
   WHY SHOULD PEOPLE FOLLOW WEIGHT WATCHERS? 8
   WHAT IS FREESTYLE? 9

CHAPTER TWO 10
   BASICS OF INSTANT POT 10
   BENEFITS OF INSTANT POT 16
   TIPS FOR CLEANING INSTANT POT 18

CHAPTER THREE 21
   FOODS TO EAT 21
   FOODS TO AVOID 24
   EXCELLENT WEIGHT WATCHERS TIPS 27

CHAPTER FOUR 31
   30 RECIPES FOR BREAKFAST 31

CHAPTER FIVE 80
   30 RECIPES FOR LUNCH 80

CHAPTER SIX 129
   30 RECIPES FOR DINNER 129

CHAPTER SEVEN 173
   10 SPECIAL RECIPES. 173

CONCLUSION 189

CHAPTER ONE
WHAT IS WEIGHT WATCHERS?

Weight Watchers is a program designed to help participant's lose weight. The program differs from others because the participants are allowed to purchase and cook their own food options. It has been proven to be effective, and is a great diet option for those who want to lose quite a bit of weight and those who may just have a few extra pounds that they would like to be rid of. Weight Watchers also has a separate program for those with special dietary needs.

Online or Face to Face

There are two ways to sign up for weight watchers. The first and more traditional way is to find and attend face-to-face meetings. Meetings are generally once a week and include discussions, updates, the sharing of resources and weekly weigh-ins. Online Weight Watchers is for those who are either uncomfortable with face to face meetings or who prefer the convenience of working with the program online. Both methods have proven to be effective.

Food Points

To make Weight Watchers work, participants share their weight loss goals, eating habits, and activity preferences. The system then generates a daily points average. This average is found by considering how much weight participants want to lose, and what the current body weight is. Every day, the participant's record the foods and quantities that they eat. These foods are assigned point values, and the goal of the participant is to remain within the average points that they are allowed for the day. This teaches participants to eat healthily and to come to an understanding of what they should avoid. For example, a cheeseburger may be 12 points. If a participant only has 20 points total for the day, then eating a cheeseburger will take up over half of their daily points. They can still eat the burger if they would like to, but in order to stick to the diet, they only have 8 points to use for all of the rest of their meals and snacks. But if that person instead had a cup of rice with a side of baked chicken and some spinach, they may only use 7 or 8 points, meaning that they can have more options for other meals. This teaches participants what foods are worse or better than others.

Those who sign up for weight watchers are also given a predetermined number of reserve points that they can use whenever they would like. These points can be added to daily totals or can be saved until the end of every week.

Activity Points

Activity points are used to reward exercise. Many different forms of exercise are considered acceptable, from running, to swimming, to gardening. The duration and intensity of these activities determines how many activity points awarded. These points can be used if bonus food points have already been depleted. The more participants stay active, the more flexible their food options are. This encourages participants to couple good eating habits with good exercise habits.

Weigh-Ins

Weight Watchers weigh-ins occur once a week. For face-to-face meetings, participants weigh themselves in front of their group members as a sort of bonding process. The weights are recorded and advice is given according to the amount of weight loss or, if applicable, weight gain, for the week. For online weigh-ins, participants enter their weights into the computer each week.

Resources

Weight Watchers offers many resources for their members. From recipes to tips and advice, members can find information on how to diet and stay healthy at the same time. Weight Watchers offers do's and don'ts on how to eat and the best ways to lose weight and establish healthy routines for many kinds of people in a variety of lifestyle situations.

Maintenance

Another unique aspect of the weight watchers program is that it teaches its participants how to keep the weight off, and how to keep up with their new healthy lifestyles and it does this while the program is still running by teaching members what is better for them to eat and why. The program becomes second nature, and instead of just providing members with pre made food, it teaches them to pick better portions and options.

BENEFITS OF WEIGHT WATCHERS.

By now, many of us must have heard of the Weight Watchers Program. The Weight Watchers Program is one of the most effective and popular weight loss plans for those who require to lose weight, and thousands have benefitted from this program. Nevertheless, this program would not fit everyone despite having plenty of advantages. This is because the very same programs also have a few limitations and drawbacks of their own. Do consider all the advantages and disadvantages of this Weight Watcher Program before a decision is made of whether to take it up.

The advantages of the plan are as stated below:

1. There is no restriction on the type of food to be consumed, thus there are no forbidden foods. This program allows you to eat anything that you want, but in moderation. The advantage of this is that you can continue to enjoy all your favourite food, nevertheless in smaller portions than before. There is no banned food list on the Weight Watcher Program, thus you do not have to worry about not being able to eat what you love.

2. Your group would be well led by a leader that is well-aware of each member's specific requirements in terms of nutritional needs, thus you would receive plenty of useful knowledge in terms of diets, eating the right food, and consuming enough water each day

3. The sessions are flexible, thus you could probably bring your children with you when you attend meeting sessions. You do not have to worry about leaving them alone at home as you strive to improve on your weight issues.

4. Achievable results are championed by the Weight Watchers Program, thus you would be able to see a slow and steady loss of weight in your body. Expect to lose at least one kilogram after one week of signing up, and more as the weeks go by. The more effort you put in, and the more disciplined you are, the more the weight that you would be able to shed.

5. Education on how to control your eating portions is provided. With the Weight Watcher Program, you would learn how to measure and track your food portions, thus even if you stop attending the sessions, the knowledge stays with you for life so that you can control your weight based on what you eat every day.

Considering the many advantages of this plan, one would do well to sign up for it. Nevertheless, ensure that the plan would fit your schedule and preferences before you opt for it to avoid disappointments.

WHY SHOULD PEOPLE FOLLOW WEIGHT WATCHERS?

"If you're looking for more information on the Weight Watchers Program then, grab a chair & buckle down, because this is the ebook that you've been looking for."

In the current situation with obesity & the amount of overweight people in the UK & USA, there couldn't be a more important time than now to focus on health issues.

There is a modern stereotype of someone sitting on the couch at home watching the television, with a remote in one hand & a large bag of crisps in the other & a few bowls of snacks on the coffee table beside you.

It seems to be a distant memory of people of all ages out walking or running & children playing sport at their local playing park or sports centre.

So what has changed in recent years?

I think the general perception of keeping fit & healthy has changed & that there isn't enough emphasis put on the subject. The more gadgets that becomes available to people, the more chances of you becoming a couch potato. You just have to look at the types of things that would prevent you from doing exercise - Games Consoles, Satellite TV, Mobile Phones, MP3 & 4 Players... These are the type of things that are causing people, especially the younger generation to stay indoors more often.

Joining a club like Weight Watchers is a huge step in the right direction, as not only will you get involved with a program with a sensible action plan, but you will be getting out of the house & meeting new people with a similar goal to yourself - losing weight & getting fitter.

WHAT IS FREESTYLE?

The new Weight Watchers Freestyle plan, which was launched in the U.S. on 12/3/17, now includes a much wider range of over 200 zero SmartPoints foods from which to base your meals and snacks including eggs, skinless chicken breast, skinless turkey breast, fish and seafood, corn, beans, peas, lentils, tofu, nonfat plain yogurt and so much more.

Previously, only fruits and vegetables had been considered zero points.

While you are always free to eat whatever you want on Weight Watchers, the Freestyle plan nudges you toward choosing nutritious foods by assigning them lower or even zero SmartPoints.

CHAPTER TWO
BASICS OF INSTANT POT

First of all, make sure to read through the manual that came with your Instant Pot. Each model is different, and some have more function buttons than others. For this guide, we'll be using the 7 in 1 IP-DUO (6qt). The manual also includes some handy tips and suggestions about the various features. And it goes into detail on how important things, like the steam release handle, work.

Now before we get into my Instant Pot guide for beginners, the first thing you need to remember is that an Instant Pot is not just a pressure cooker. It can also sauté (like a frying pan) and cook things slowly (like a slow cooker). Getting additional accessories like a steam basket or small springform cake pan makes it even more versatile (because yes, you can even make cake in the Instant Pot!).

Also remember that an Instant Pot isn't exactly instant. While the cook times for most foods in the Instant Pot are amazingly short, your Instant Pot will also need time to get up to pressure, and time to release that pressure. So something with a 10 minute cook time could actually take 25 minutes from start to finish. But still, most of that time passes without you having to actively interact with the

Instant Pot, so compared to cooking on a stove top, you're still saving a lot of time!

One last thing before I start this Instant Pot guide for beginners- be aware that many foods are best cooked with additional liquid (water or broth) added. The Instant Pot needs this to create the appropriate steam to cook your food fully. Thick liquids (like cream of soups) don't count. Dairy also doesn't pressure cook well.

The Instant Pot's Basic Controls

This wouldn't be a good Instant Pot guide for beginners if we didn't discuss the basic controls! Below is a picture of the control panel for the IP we're using for this guide:

Underneath your Instant Pot's LED display is a section that says "Low Pressure" and "High Pressure." The pressure button changes these when you're doing a manual program.

Under the pressure indicators is an area that says "Less | Normal | More." These are called the mode indicators. The "Adjust" button changes these. This will affect the cook time. You can't use the Adjust button for the Rice or Manual functions.

Under the mode indicators are a minus symbol and a plus symbol. You can push the minus or plus to manually adjust the cook time. You can change the cook time for all the function buttons except for the "Rice" function. This is important because different foods of the same category (like different beans) take a different amount of time to cook.

Below that are the "Adjust," "Timer," "Manual," and "Keep Warm/Cancel" buttons (the exact location of these buttons may vary a little across different Instant Pot models). I already covered the "Adjust" button and will discuss "Manual" in a bit.

The Timer button is used to delay when the Instant Pot starts heating up and working. So if you set a timer for 1 hour, it'll start warming up in 1 hour, then go through the cook time you specified. Don't use it for perishable foods that can go bad if left out at room temperature (like raw meat) or foods with a porridge-type consistency (they could mess up the float valve and overflow if left alone).

The Keep Warm/Cancel button can do either of the two things in its name. If your Instant Pot is running a cook program, pushing this button cancels it and puts the machine on standby. If the Instant Pot is on standby, pushing this turns on the keep warm program to keep your food warm until you're ready to eat it. The Instant Pot will automatically go into keep warm mode after it finishes cooking.

Now let's get down to the meat of this Instant Pot guide for beginners… the function buttons!

The Instant Pot's Function Buttons

Manual

I'm going to start this section of my Instant Pot how-to guide off with the manual button. It's not technically classified as a function button, but I think it should be. I like it because it's the one that gives you the most control. With this button you get to choose whether you cook your food at high or low pressure, and you can set your own cook time. If any of the preset buttons don't work as you'd like, just go with the manual button! Once you become more used to working with your Instant Pot, you may decide to use this button most of the time.

Sauté

The sauté button is another button you'll probably wind up using a lot. It saves you from dirtying a frying pan just to brown foods first (like you would have to do with a slow cooker). For best flavor, it's usually a good idea to sauté your meats a bit first. You could also use this setting to sauté additional ingredients, like onions and bell peppers.

Soup

The soup button is for cooking liquids like soup (obviously), and also broth. What's great about this function is that it makes the Instant Pot hot enough to get your liquid simmering, but not scalding hot. This way your soup ingredients don't get too broken down.

Meat/Stew

This preset meat button is for non-poultry meats like beef and pork. It's also for cooking thick stew-type meals. Use the Adjust button to change the final texture of the meat. Set your Instant Pot to the More setting if you want the meat to be very tender and more broken down.

Bean/Chili

Did you know that you can cook dry beans in your Instant Pot? It's a great way to save money, compared with buying canned beans (especially if you eat organic). You can use this setting to cook your raw beans, or you could use it to cook bean-based dishes (like chili). I'd suggest using the Adjust button to set your Instant Pot to the More setting for thoroughly cooked, tender beans.

Poultry

This handy button will quickly become your favorite if you love chicken! You can even use it to cook frozen chicken if you forgot to defrost it. Use the Adjust button to change the final texture of the chicken, or to adjust the cook time for more or less chicken in the pot.

Rice

The rice button essentially gives your Instant Pot the ability to also be a rice cooker. As mentioned earlier, you can't change the cook time for this function. Your Instant Pot will set its own time based on how heavy your rice is. The rice can be raw or parboiled.

Multigrain

This Instant Pot function is one of the more complex ones. It's designed, as it says, for multigrains. So if you're cooking wild rice, brown rice, quinoa, lentils, and other hardy grains (or mixtures of several of those grains), then you'll want to use this function. If you press the "More" button, the Instant Pot will include soak time, which is handy if your grain requires it. This setting does take some time, though. "Normal" is 40 minutes of active cooking time, "Less" is 20 minutes, and "More" is 45 minutes of soaking + 1 hour of cooking.

Porridge

I've seen this button have different names for different models, but it's the same idea. It will make porridge out of grains like oats or rice. Use the "Normal" mode for rice porridge, and the "More" mode for porridge made of other types of grain or beans. With this setting you have to use the natural release or else your porridge could splatter out of the steam release.

Steam

This function is the best for cooking crisp veggies! It's also great for seafood. You'll want to use this one with plenty of additional liquid, and put your food in the steam rack or buy a steam basket to use. And at the end, use the quick release. The natural release will take too long and the food will wind up overcooked.

Slow Cook

We're nearing the end of my Instant Pot Guide for beginners, but I don't want you to go without knowing about this handy feature. It essentially allows you to use your Instant Pot like your slow cooker! Use the plus and minus buttons to change the time, and use the Adjust button to change the heat level. Not every slow cooker recipe can convert to an Instant Pot set to "Slow Cook," but it's definitely worth a try!

Yogurt

If your Instant Pot has this feature, you can use it as a yogurt maker! You can either make it straight in the Instant Pot's inner pot or you can make your yogurt in glass jars. There are several steps to this process, so if you're interested in this, you'll want to consult your model's manual.

And there you have it! Now you're ready to go try your first Instant Pot recipe. Have fun!

BENEFITS OF INSTANT POT

There are a lot of reasons to love Instant Pot! The main reasons are:

Fewer dirty dishes – Since you can sauté and pressure cook in one pot, you can make almost any dish a one-pot dinner

Lower electric bill – An Instant Pot uses far less energy than your oven or stove, so over time, you spend much less on electricity

Faster meals – Pressure cooking cooks many foods very quickly (sometimes up to 70% faster!)

Easier meals – Once you've added all the ingredients and sealed the lid, you can set and forget! The Instant Pot will automatically turn off and switch to warm mode when cook time is complete

Healthier meals – Because you only need to add enough water to create steam for pressure, most of the nutrients in the food are retained

Comfortable kitchen – All the heat is trapped inside the Instant Pot while your food is cooking so unlike your oven or stove, your kitchen won't heat up while dinner is cooking.

TIPS FOR CLEANING INSTANT POT

While the pots don't give up easily, yet if they are not properly maintained then you are sure to see a change in its overall efficiency. A little different from your traditional cleaning methods, instant pots are easy to maintain, and here's how you can clean your instant pot.

Off and Cool

Before you start on, make sure your instant pot is unplugged and has cooled down. You don't want to work with a partially heated instant pot. Once cooled, separate the lid, the inner pot and the steamer rack. It is best to get all the parts out so that you can deep clean every little part and area.

The Exterior Body

For the exterior, never immerse it in water. The exterior body is made of electronic components and cleaning with a damp cloth is your best bet. You can use the same damp cloth for cleaning the inside of the body too. For the cracks, you can use a small toothbrush to get into those deep cracks and remove dried food debris.

The Lid

You can clean the lid by placing it in the dish washer, but regular cleaning with water can do the trick as well. In case you are in deep-clean mode, remove the sealing ring, the anti-block shield, the steam-release handle and the float valve and then clean the lid. Once done, reattach the steam release handle and float valve, and make sure both these work normally without any obstruction. While cleaning the lid, make sure to not remove the steam valve. Once the anti-block shield comes off, you have access to clean it easily.

The Steam-Release and Float Valve

For the steam release handle and float valve, its best if you hand wash it with small brushes. That ought to get most of the debris, all while being gentle on the tiny equipment.

The Sealing Ring

Because the sealing ring makes sure that the pressure stays inside while cooking, it usually takes a lot of beating. Therefore, if you notice the ring to be cracked or deformed, you can always get a new one. However, if you wish to clean the one you have, soaking it in vinegar will give you the best result because it gets rid of the residual food odor.

The Interior Pot and Steam Rack

The interior pot and the steam rack both can be cleaned and washed like all other utensils, either using dishwasher or by hand washing. But despite the regular cleaning, sometimes the odor tends to stay. The easiest way to get rid of that pesky odor and rusty stains is by soaking the lid in one cup of vinegar. After five minutes, drain out the vinegar, wash it with water, rub in some soft bristles, and it will be good as new. But be careful, Never use steel wool for cleaning the inside. NEVER.

The Steam-Clean Hack

If you are in the mood for a quick but neat clean-up, then here's a quick hack. Instead of dissembling everything, take your instant pot, add in 2 cups of vinegar or 2 cups of water with cut-out lemons and run the steam program for 2 minutes. This gets rid of the odor and stains inside the internal pot and sealing ring. Be sure to let it all air-dry afterwards.

Despite how hard they tend to work, instant pots are easy to clean. It only requires some basic knowledge of dissembling and assembling, and some quick tricks up your sleeve.

CHAPTER THREE
FOODS TO EAT

Along with exercise, you will need to find the best foods to eat to lose weight. Consuming a diet balanced with the right nutrition, but one with fewer calories will help the pounds to start dropping off, allowing you to reach your weight loss goal. If you are tired of carrying around excessive weight and desperately want to do something about it, then today is the day to start.

Getting started with any weight loss plan can be difficult. After all, you have so many choices when it comes to exercise, equipment, and diet that it sometimes seems confusing. We want you to be successful and most importantly, healthy. Therefore, we have pulled a list together for you on the ten best foods to eat to lose weight. Remember, the key with any weight loss is to be consistent, determined, and dedicated. Then, choosing the right exercise program and changing your diet will push you to success.

Salad Now, the key to salad being one of the foods to eat to lose weight is not becoming carried away with all the fillers. Instead, create your salad from several lettuce varieties, fresh tomato, cucumber, carrot, cabbage, celery, and beetroot, which are all low calories ingredients. Then, be careful when choosing the dressing in that this is what has all the calories. Choose only low-fat dressings or lemon, with salt and pepper.

Grapes Another one of the best foods to eat to lose weight, grapes are great fresh or frozen. These tiny pieces of fruit are low in calories, delicious, and make an excellent snack.

Oranges This type of citrus food is also a great snack. Considering that an average size orange only has 50 calories while providing a sweet, juicy treat, you can see why this is among the top 10 foods to eat to lose weight.

Potatoes For some reason, most people think that potatoes have to be avoided at all costs when trying to lose weight. In reality, potatoes are rich in vitamins and nutrients, as well as being low calorie. As long as you stick with boiled or baked potatoes without the heavy sour cream and butter, you will do fine. Toppings that will add flavor but not calories include salsa, low-fat cheese, and even cottage cheese.

High Fiber Cereals In addition to making you feel full, cereals high in fiber are low in calories. For instance, you could choose white rice, corn, or oats, which are delicious and filling.

Sweet Potatoes These potatoes are still low in calories, having about 120 each. Again, as long as you boil or bake them, sweet potatoes are creamy and satisfying, while also being rich in vitamins. Because of this, we wanted to list sweet potatoes in our list of foods to eat to lose weight.

Popcorn The key here is to eat only air-popped popcorn. With this, the popcorn is popped using air instead of rich butter. By adding a little bit of salt, you have a wonderful snack.

Egg Whites You can enjoy a breakfast of scrambled egg whites, which are high in protein and low in calories. Using low-fat butter or spray cooking oil and a little seasoning, you will find these to be quite tasty, making this yet another great choice of food to eat to lose weight.

Bananas and Blueberries The average banana has only 60 calories. Bananas are also filling, while being loaded with vitamins. Additionally, you could enjoy an entire 12-ounce bag of unsweetened blueberries for just 80 calories. To sweeten them, you could use an artificial sweetener such as NutraSweet or Splenda As you can see, both of these fruits are considered a great food to eat to lose weight.

Mango and Papaya In the dried form, papaya and mango are ideal snacks, especially when craving something sweet. Both are a great source of vitamin C, vitamin A, and iron. These are also among the best considerations for food to eat to lose weight.

The goal in changing diet to lose weight is to make better food choices. However, you also need to know that on occasion, you should allow yourself a special treat such as a candy bar or piece of cake. Studies have shown that diets that cut all favorite foods out are destined to fail. Therefore, know it is okay to have a special food once in a while.

FOODS TO AVOID

Your gout and the foods you eat are related. Here, you'll discover a simple list of foods to avoid with gout to help you lower uric acid levels and prevent gout.

Just how are your gout and the food you eat related? First off, your gout is caused by crystals that have formed in your joints and surrounding tissue. These are formed when you have high levels of uric acid in your blood. And uric acid is produced when chemical compounds called 'purines' breakdown during the normal metabolizing process in your body.

No problem, because your kidneys process and excrete excess uric acid out of your body. But if your kidneys just aren't functioning as well as they might, or, your body is producing too much uric acid for your kidneys to handle, then excess levels of uric acid are retained in your body. To prevent gout you need to reduce your uric acid.

Now, purines are also present in food at varying degrees of concentrations or levels. The objective is to reduce or avoid those with high purine levels and replace with those foods that have relatively low levels.

As a rule of thumb, high purine foods are also high animal protein foods. But even some vegetables and legumes can have high levels in them. The list of these types of food is too long to go into here, but here's a summary list of foods to avoid with gout...

- shellfish (e.g. mussels, scallops, shrimp)
- some fish (e.g. herring, mackerel, anchovies, salmon)
- organ meats (e.g. liver, kidneys, heart)
- gravy, broth, consomme, etc.
- poultry (e.g. duck, turkey)
- game (venison, pheasant, grouse)
- fatty red meat (burgers, mincemeat, meat extracts)
- yeast (baker's, brewer's, yeast extracts)
- dried legumes (e.g. peas, beans, lentils)
- some vegetables (e.g. cauliflower, asparagus, mushrooms, spinach)

By avoiding some of these altogether, and perhaps reducing your intake of others, you can help to reduce and manage your uric acid at healthier levels. The problem is that each person's metabolism is different, and what may cause one person a problem, may not cause another person.

For example, I can seem to eat shrimps and prawns okay, but I know somebody who only needs to 'look' at those to trigger a gout attack! So you need to figure out what your safe and unsafe foods are yourself. Keeping a daily food diary is an excellent way to record the outcomes of your daily diet.

Keep in mind though, that you also need to face up to the other key issues that affect your ability to eliminate your gout for good; as well as your diet, you have your weight position, your lifestyle, family history, etc.

And it uses fully-researched, totally natural methods. So that you benefit two ways: (1) you get rid of your excruciating pain very fast, and, (2) you prevent your gout returning, so that you reduce the risk of permanent damage.

EXCELLENT WEIGHT WATCHERS TIPS

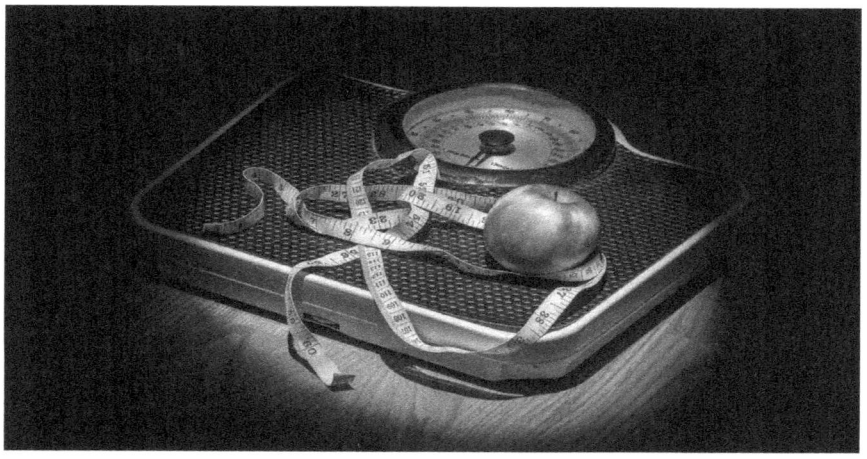

Top 15 Way To Make Weight Watchers Work For You

Weight Watchers Tips & Tricks

I have to say that the years that I've been on and off Weight Watchers, it has ALWAYS worked for me! But it definitely requires some hard work and commitment.

1. Keep A Journal - This is a definite must! There is no way to keep track of everything without one. You must update your journal with all the foods/drinks you consume on a daily basis. Most of the time we tend to forget those few snacks that we had throughout the day. By always having your journal handy, write it down immediately whether it be just a few cookies or just a glass of wine.

2. Liquids - It's a great idea to always have a bottle of water with you all the time. This way you can just sip on water all day. And before you know it, you'll eventually have the 6 glasses of water that you should intake in 1 day. Sometimes when you feel hunger, it's not actually that you need food. You may just need some water.

So this is a great tip if you just ate a snack, but it didn't quite fill your hunger. Being hydrated helps! And if water doesn't quite do it for you, have a diet soda, which it a little more sweet and may be more fulfilling than a plain old glass of water.

3. Food/Snacks - Find those low point snacks and stick to them! They will help throughout the day when you feel your belly asking you for some food. I personally like to have apples and carrots at work and home. Of course you don't need to only eat these. But that's just what I like for a low or zero point snack. It's OK to indulge in some sweets now and then, but make sure you know how many points that chocolate bar is.

4. Grocery Shopping - MAKE A LIST! And before you go grocery shopping, make sure you know the points values of the foods you buy before going to the supermarket. It's a good idea to write down the points values of the items you're going to by next to each item on your list. If something isn't on your list that you found in the supermarket, be sure to read those labels and serving sizes. Calculate those points!

5. Cooking - I like to stick to the healthier choices when cooking. For example, use I Can't Believe it's not butter instead of regular butter. Use fat free items such as fat free chicken broth. If you're having salad, there are many fat free dressings available in all types of varieties. Just be smart!

6. Weighing/Measuring Foods - Buy a scale! I recommend the Weight Watchers scale. It weighs in grams and in ounces. Of course you can use other scales, I just prefer to use the Weight Watchers scale. It's actually quite shocking to see a 4 oz. piece of steak on your plate and see how small it actually is.

7. Eating Out - Make healthy choices. If you do indulge yourself in your favorite dish that's 20+ points, a good thing to do is ask for a container as soon as you get your food. Put half into the container and save it for lunch tomorrow. And if you must have that piece of cheesecake for dessert, why not share with your friend instead of eating the entire slice yourself! And remember to follow my restaurant guide for the points and points plus values.

8. Friends & Family - Make sure to find a companion along the way to help you with your weight loss journey, even if this friend isn't on weight watchers. It makes it so much easier to stay on track if you have someone by your side rather than on your own. Tell your family you're on a diet so they don't force the extra helping of mashed potatoes on you!

9. Use The Calculator - Make some informed decisions and use the points calculator to figure out exactly how many points something is and don't just guess. Knowing how many points something is will help you make that decision if you think you are still hungry and want something more.

10. Exercise - This is one of the most important things to do if you want to shed those pounds even quicker. I know it's hard to go out and actually do it. But if you have your mind set and want to lose weight, this is the best thing for your body and health! It helps you not only lose weight but it with burn fat, build some muscle and even eat a little something extra with since you get a few additional points if you exercise. These are called Activity Points and these can be added to your daily intake. So the more you exercise, the more points you can get and the more you can eat! Of course, just be smart and don't think after an hour of exercising you should go home and eat whatever you want. All that exercising you just did, was worthless if you do this. It may help to eat a small protein within a half hour after exercising. This will help your body's metabolism work better.

11. Meetings/Support Groups - These will definitely help you along your journey. You can share your stories with other members and see how they're doing compared to you. It's not a contest, so don't get down on yourself if others are shedding pounds quicker than you. At these meetings be sure to talk to everyone and you'll get some great ideas for everything from low point snacks, to great restaurants to eat at. If you're doing this on your own and at home, join some forums and share your stories.

12. Weigh Ins - The dreaded weekly weigh-ins. I know it's hard to see that you only lost 1 pound or even gained 1 pound after eating healthy the entire week and exercising. Don't get discouraged and stick to it. Maybe you can try to change a few things that you've been eating. Or if you haven't been exercising, start!. But, once you get in the groove, you'll be eating better, and feeling healthier and those pounds will start falling off! Trust me!

13. Diet? - Don't think of yourself as always being on a diet. This is a lifestyle change! This is actually how you should be eating. Once you learn that, you'll feel as if you're not even dieting. If you feel like you're on a diet, you're already setting yourself up for failure. And once you know the points values right off the top of your head, it doesn't even feel like it's a diet. It become routine.

14. Just Live Your Life - Again, if you feel your dieting, it's not going to work. I know when you first start "dieting" you seem to be hungry ALL THE TIME. This will change once you get used to your new lifestyle. It's all about choices. Make the right choices for the foods you eat and when you go out to a restaurant. It's in your own hands.

15. The New You - You've stuck with it and it's working! That's great! Now keep it up and stay on track!

CHAPTER FOUR
30 RECIPES FOR BREAKFAST
BREAKFAST

1

Skinny Beef Taco Rice Skillet

Ingredients

- 2 cup beef stock
- 1 cup long-grain white rice
- 1 lb extra-lean ground beef
- 1 large red onion, finely chopped
- 1 green bell pepper, finely chopped
- 3/4 cup frozen corn
- 1/2 cup water
- 1 packet (1 1/4 oz) taco seasoning mix
- 1 1/2 cup fresh salsa
- 1 fresh cilantro, chopped, optional

Directions

- Prep 10 min
- Cook 25 min
- Ready 35 min
- Add beef stock to a saucepan and bring to a boil. Add rice, cover, and cook until done, about 25 minutes.
- While the rice is cooking, brown ground beef in a non-stick skillet, about 3 minutes. Add onion and bell pepper and cook, stirring occasionally, for 7 minutes. Add corn and cook for 3 more minutes. Add water and taco seasoning mix. Turn down the heat and cook until the meat is done and the liquid is almost completely absorbed, 5-10 minutes.

- When rice is cooked, stir it into the meat and vegetables. Turn off the heat and mix in salsa. Garnish with cilantro, if desired.

Nutritional Information

Serving Size: 1 (513 g)

Servings Per Recipe: 3

Amount Per Serving

Calories 601 Calories from Fat 83

% Daily Value

Total Fat 9g 14%

Saturated Fat 4g 19%

Cholesterol 94mg 31%

Sodium 2435mg 101%

Total Carbohydrate 88g 29%

Dietary Fiber 9g 34%

Sugars 9g 37%

Protein 44g 87%

2

Barbecue Meatloaf

Ingredients

- 1 lb 93% lean ground beef
- 1/2 cup barbecue sauce, divided
- 1/4 cup frozen chopped onion, pressed dry
- 1/4 cup seasoned Italian bread crumbs

- 2 large egg white

Directions

- Prep 5 min
- Cook 40 min
- Ready 45 min
- Preheat oven to 375°F.
- Combine meat, 1/4 cup barbecue sauce, onion, breadcrumbs, egg whites, and seasons of your choice in a large bowl; stir well.
- Shape mixture into a loaf pan. Spread remaining 1/4 cup barbecue sauce over loaf.
- Bake at 375°F for 40 minutes or until desired degree of doneness.

Nutritional Information

Serving Size: 1 (168 g)

Servings Per Recipe: 4

Amount Per Serving

Calories 240 Calories from Fat 55

% Daily Value

Total Fat 6g 9%

Saturated Fat 3g 13%

Cholesterol 70mg 23%

Sodium 499mg 20%

Total Carbohydrate 17g 5%

Dietary Fiber 1g 2%

Sugars 9g 34%

Protein 27g 54%

3

Ground Beef and Cabbage Casserole

Ingredients

- 1 lb lean ground beef
- 1/2 cup onion, chopped
- 1/2 cup brown rice, uncooked
- 1 cup tomato sauce
- 1 1/2 tsp beef bouillon
- 1 tbsp Worcestershire sauce
- 1 tsp sugar
- 1/2 tsp dried dill
- 3/4 cup water
- 4 1/2 cup cabbage, coarsely chopped
- 6 oz cheese, swiss, or Colby, shredded

Directions

- Prep 15 min
- Cook 100 min
- Ready 115 min
- Brown meat and onion and season to taste.
- Put cabbage in greased 9x13 pan. Sprinkle rice over cabbage. Sprinkle meat and onion over cabbage.
- Mix tomato sauce, bouillon, Worcestershire, sugar, dill and water. Pour over cabbage mixture.
- Bake, covered at 350F for 1 1/2 hours.
- Remove from oven and sprinkle cheese over top. Let sit until cheese is melted.

Nutritional Information

Serving Size: 1 (194 g)

Servings Per Recipe: 8

Amount Per Serving

Calories 249 Calories from Fat 108

% Daily Value

Total Fat 12g 18%

Saturated Fat 6g 30%

Cholesterol 56mg 18%

Sodium 271mg 11%

Total Carbohydrate 16g 5%

Dietary Fiber 2g 8%

Sugars 4g 16%

Protein 19g 38%

4

Crock Pot Lasagna

Ingredients

- 1 lb lean ground beef
- 1 onion, chopped
- 1 clove garlic, minced
- 1 can (28 oz) tomato, crushed
- 1 can (15 oz) tomato sauce
- 1 tsp salt
- 1 tsp dried oregano
- 1/2 tsp dried basil
- 1/4 tsp red pepper flakes
- 1 cup part-skim ricotta cheese
- 1 1/2 cup low-fat mozzarella cheese, shredded
- 6 lasagna noodle

- 1/2 cup parmesan cheese, shredded

Directions

- Prep 20 min
- Cook 360 min
- Ready 380 min
- In a large skillet over medium-high heat, cook ground beef, onion, and garlic, stirring to break up any chunks, until the meat is brown, 5-10 minutes. Stir in crushed tomatoes, tomato sauce, salt, dried oregano, dried basil, and red pepper flakes and simmer for another 5 minutes.
- In a small bowl, mix together ricotta and 1 cup mozzarella.
- Spoon 1/3 of the meat sauce into a slow cooker. Break 3 lasagna noodles in half, arrange them on top of the meat sauce, and top with 1/2 of the cheese mixture. Repeat with second layer. Finish with remaining 1/3 of the meat mixture. Cover and cook on Low for 4-6 hours.
- In a small bowl, combine remaining 1/2 cup mozzarella and parmesan cheese. Sprinkle over the lasagna and set aside for 10 minutes or until cheese melts and lasagna is firm.

Nutritional Information

Serving Size: 1 (372 g)

Servings Per Recipe: 6

Amount Per Serving

Calories 360 Calories from Fat 125

% Daily Value

Total Fat 14g 21%

Saturated Fat 7g 33%

Cholesterol 69mg 23%

Sodium 999mg 41%

Total Carbohydrate 31g 10%

Dietary Fiber 4g 15%

Sugars 8g 32%

Protein 28g 56%

5
Pita Pizza

Ingredients

- 1 large thin pita bread
- 1/4 cup pizza sauce
- 1/4 cup mushrooms, sliced
- 1/4 cup green pepper, chopped
- 10 small black olives, chopped
- 1/2 cup fat free mozzarella cheese
- 2 tsp parmesan cheese

- 1 pinch pizza seasoning , or oregano

Directions

- Prep 10 min
- Cook 2 min
- Ready 12 min
- Preheat oven to broil.
- Spread pizza sauce on the pita. Layer vegetables first so they are held together by the cheese. Top with mozzarella, parmesan cheese, and seasoning.
- Spray cooking spray lightly over the cheese.
- Broil for 2 minutes or until cheese is mostly melted.

Nutritional Information

Serving Size: 1 (269 g)

Servings Per Recipe: 1

Amount Per Serving

Calories 341 Calories from Fat 53

% Daily Value

Total Fat 6g 9%

Saturated Fat 1g 7%

Cholesterol 15mg 4%

Sodium 1146mg 47%

Total Carbohydrate 45g 15%

Dietary Fiber 5g 21%

Sugars 4g 15%

Protein 27g 54%

6
Easy 20 Minute Chili

Ingredients

- 1 lb lean ground beef or ground turkey
- 1 small onion, chopped
- 1 clove garlic, minced
- 1 1/2 cup water or beef stock
- 1 tbsp chili powder
- 1 tsp salt
- 16 oz canned chili beans, undrained (use hot if you like spicy chili)
- 6 oz can tomato paste

Directions

- Prep 5 min
- Cook 15 min
- Ready 20 min
- Cook Meat, onion, and garlic in a dutch oven or large saucepan on medium high heat until browned, stirring to crumble the meat well.
- Drain in a colander and rinse with hot water, return to pan. Stir in water (or stock) and remaining ingredients.
- Cover, reduce heat, and simmer 15 minutes, stirring occasionally.

Nutritional Information

Serving Size: 1 (253 g)

Servings Per Recipe: 6

Amount Per Serving

Calories 278 Calories from Fat 74

% Daily Value

Total Fat 8g 12%

Saturated Fat 3g 16%

Cholesterol 49mg 16%

Sodium 867mg 36%

Total Carbohydrate 28g 9%

Dietary Fiber 6g 23%

Sugars 4g 17%

Protein 24g 47%

Mexican Casserole

Ingredients

- 1 lb extra lean ground beef
- 1/2 cup onion, chopped
- 1/4 cup sliced jalapeno pepper, chopped
- 2 cup fresh tomato, chopped (or one 15 oz can diced tomatoes)
- 1 can (15 oz) corn, kernels drained
- 1 can (15 oz) black beans, rinsed and drained
- 1 package (1 1/4 oz) taco seasoning mix
- 8 corn tortilla
- 3/4 cup nonfat sour cream
- 1/3 cup reduced-fat shredded Mexican cheese blend
- 1/3 bunch fresh cilantro, chopped, to taste (less or more)

Directions

- Prep 25 min

- Cook 25 min
- Ready 50 min
* Brown ground beef and chopped onions in large skillet; brown 10 to 12 minutes or until thoroughly cooked, stirring constantly. Drain well and rinse with warm water to remove all fat; return beef/onions to skillet.
* Add corn, black beans, tomatoes, jalapenos, and taco seasoning mix; mix well. Reduce heat; simmer 5 minutes.
* Meanwhile spray 12 x 8 inch (2 quart) baking dish with nonstick cooking spray. Cut each tortilla in half; place 8 halves in bottom of sprayed baking dish, overlapping slightly.
* Spoon half of beef mixture evenly over tortillas. Spoon sour cream over beef mixture; spread evenly. Top with remaining 8 tortilla halves and remaining beef mixture. (Cover tightly with foil & freeze for later or cook as directed below).
* Thaw overnight if frozen. Preheat oven to 350°F. Bake for 25 minutes. Remove from oven and sprinkle with cheese. Cover; let stand 5 minutes or until cheese is melted. Sprinkle with chopped cilantro and serve.

Nutritional Information

Serving Size: 1 (346 g)

Servings Per Recipe: 6

Amount Per Serving

Calories 355 Calories from Fat 52

% Daily Value

Total Fat 6g 9%

Saturated Fat 2g 11%

Cholesterol 50mg 16%

Sodium 815mg 33%

Total Carbohydrate 52g 17%

Dietary Fiber 10g 41%

Sugars 8g 32%

Protein 27g 53%

8

Lasagna with Meat Sauce

Ingredients

- 9 lasagna noodles
- 1 tsp fennel seeds
- 1 tsp olive oil
- 1/2 lb lean ground beef, 10% or less fat
- 1 onion, chopped
- 1 red bell pepper, seeded and chopped
- 1 zucchini, chopped
- 2 container (15 oz each) refrigerated marinara sauce
- 1 1/2 cup fat-free ricotta cheese
- 1/2 cup part-skim mozzarella cheese, shredded
- 1/4 cup pecorino romano cheese, grated

Directions

- Prep 20 min
- Cook 50 min
- Ready 70 min
- Cook lasagna noodles according to package directions. Drain, rinse with cold water, and set aside.
- Toast fennel seeds by placing them in a small dry skillet over medium-low heat. Cook, shaking the pan and stirring constantly, until lightly browned and fragrant, 2 to 3

- minutes. Watch seeds carefully so they do not burn. Remove from the pan, cool, and grind to a powder.
- Heat olive oil in a large nonstick skillet over medium-high heat. Add ground beef, onion, bell pepper, and zucchini. Cook, stirring occasionally, until the beef has browned. Stir in marinara sauce and fennel, then bring to a boil. Reduce heat and simmer uncovered until slightly thickened and flavors are blended, about 10 minutes.
- Preheat oven to 375 degrees F (190 degrees C).
- Spread 1/4 of the meat sauce in a 13 x 9 inch baking dish. Top with 3 lasagna noodles, then spread with 1/2 cup ricotta cheese. Repeat the layers twice, ending with the meat sauce. Cover with foil and bake for 30 minutes. Remove foil and sprinkle with mozzarella and pecorino romano cheeses. Bake until heated through and cheeses are lightly browned, about 20 more minutes. Let stand for about 10 minutes before serving.

Nutritional Information

Serving Size: 1 (242 g)

Servings Per Recipe: 8

Amount Per Serving

Calories 287 Calories from Fat 80

% Daily Value

Total Fat 9g 13%

Saturated Fat 3g 15%

Cholesterol 28mg 9%

Sodium 675mg 28%

Total Carbohydrate 36g 11%

Dietary Fiber 2g 8%

Sugars 13g 50%

Protein 15g 30%

9

Pizza Casserole

Ingredients

- 1 lb 96% lean ground beef
- 1 medium onion, chopped
- 1 can (16 oz) tomato sauce
- 1/2 tsp dried basil
- 3 garlic cloves, minced
- 1 tsp Italian seasoning
- 1/2 cup mushrooms, sliced
- 1/2 cup bell pepper, diced
- 1/2 cup tomato, diced
- 16 oz refrigerated biscuit dough, should be 8 biscuits per can
- 1 1/4 cup fat-free mozzarella cheese, shredded

Directions

- Prep 10 min
- Cook 40 min
- Ready 50 min
- Preheat oven to 350.
- In skillet, brown meat over medium heat, stirring to crumble.
- Stir in onion, tomato sauce, basil, garlic, and Italian seasoning.
- Add veggies
- Add quartered biscuit dough to the pan of sauce & meat; stir gently until biscuits are covered with sauce.

- Spray a 9 x 13" casserole dish with cooking spray. Dump the mixture into the dish.
- Bake for 25 minutes.
- Sprinkle with cheese, and bake an additional 10 minutes or until biscuits are done.
- Let stand 5 minutes before serving.

Nutritional Information

Serving Size: 1 (343 g)

Servings Per Recipe: 8

Amount Per Serving

Calories 335 Calories from Fat 102

% Daily Value

Total Fat 11g 17%

Saturated Fat 3g 17%

Cholesterol 38mg 12%

Sodium 1186mg 49%

Total Carbohydrate 35g 11%

Dietary Fiber 3g 11%

Sugars 9g 35%

Protein 23g 45%

Mexican Quinoa Casserole

Ingredients

- 1 cup quinoa
- 2 tsp olive oil
- 1 lb extra lean ground beef
- 1 small onion, chopped
- 1 to 2 garlic cloves
- 1 tsp coriander
- 2 tsp chili powder
- 2 tsp oregano
- 4 to 6 dashes hot sauce
- 1 can (14 oz) corn, drained
- 1 can (19 oz) black beans, rinsed
- 1 can (28 oz) whole tomatoes, broken up by hand
- 1 cup salsa
- 3/4 cup soy cheese

Directions

- Prep 20 min
- Cook 25 min
- Ready 45 min

* Prepare Quinoa: Rinse in a sieve under running water. Dry Roast in a skillet for approximately 7 minutes until a crackling sound is heard. Boil 1.5 cups of water in a small saucepan, add the dry roasted quinoa. Turn down the heat to low, cover and simmer for 20 minutes.
* While quinoa is simmering, heat oil in large skillet. Add garlic and chopped onions, cook 2 or 3 minutes.
* Add beef, spices and hot sauce. You may want to add a little salt and pepper here also. Brown.
* Spread quinoa in a large baking dish.
* Layer remaining ingredients in this order: Beef, corn, tomatoes, salsa, black beans and finally the grated soy cheese (Jalapeño flavor recommended).
* Bake at 450°F for 20 minutes. Broil for an additional 3-5 minutes to turn the cheese golden.

Nutritional Information

Serving Size: 1 (235 g)

Servings Per Recipe: 8

Amount Per Serving

Calories 303 Calories from Fat 59

% Daily Value

Total Fat 7g 10%

Saturated Fat 2g 9%

Cholesterol 35mg 11%

Sodium 57mg 2%

Total Carbohydrate 41g 13%

Dietary Fiber 9g 34%

Sugars 6g 22%

Protein 22g 44%

11

Quick Mexican Skillet

Ingredients

- 1 lb extra-lean ground beef
- 1 cup onion, chopped
- 1 can (14 oz) diced tomatoes, drained
- 1 1/2 cup frozen corn
- 1 can (15 oz) black beans, drained and rinsed
- 1 tsp red pepper flakes
- 1 cup fat-free sour cream
- 1/2 cup low-fat cheddar cheese, shredded

Directions

- Prep 5 min
- Cook 25 min
- Ready 30 min
- Brown ground beef and onions in a large skillet until thoroughly cooked. Mix in tomatoes, corn, back beans, and red pepper flakes. Simmer for 10 minutes, stirring occasionally. Mix in sour cream and simmer for another 10 minutes. Sprinkle with cheddar cheese before serving.

Nutritional Information

Serving Size: 1 (326 g)

Servings Per Recipe: 4

Amount Per Serving

Calories 509 Calories from Fat 82

% Daily Value

Total Fat 9g 14%

Saturated Fat 4g 20%

Cholesterol 79mg 26%

Sodium 219mg 9%

Total Carbohydrate 66g 22%

Dietary Fiber 13g 53%

Sugars 9g 36%

Protein 44g 88%

12

Taco Soup

Ingredients

- 1 lb extra lean ground beef, or turkey
- 1 large onion, diced
- 2 can (15 oz each) chili beans
- 1 can (15 oz) zesty chili beans, such as S&W
- 1 can (15 oz) black beans, drained
- 1 can (15 oz) corn, undrained
- 1 can (15 oz) tomato sauce
- 1 1/2 cup water
- 1 can (4 1/2 oz) diced green chiles
- 1 package (1 1/4 oz) taco seasoning mix
- 1 package (1 oz) ranch salad dressing mix

Directions

- Prep 5 min
- Cook 30 min
- Ready 35 min
* Brown meat and onion in a large pot, then drain any excess fat. Add both cans of chili beans, black beans, corn, tomato sauce, water, green chilies, taco seasoning, and ranch dressing mix. Bring to a boil, then reduce heat and simmer for 30 minutes.

Nutritional Information

Serving Size: 1 (261 g)

Servings Per Recipe: 12

Amount Per Serving

Calories 249   Calories from Fat 27

% Daily Value

Total Fat 3g 4%

Saturated Fat 1g 5%

Cholesterol 23mg 7%

Sodium 622mg 25%

Total Carbohydrate 39g 13%

Dietary Fiber 8g 33%

Sugars 5g 20%

Protein 19g 37%

13

Stuffed Mushroom Casserole

Ingredients

- 16 oz mushrooms (sliced)
- 2 stalks celery (diced)
- 1 medium onion (diced)
- 3 garlic cloves (minced)
- 1 cup whole wheat Panko breadcrumbs
- 2 oz Parmesan cheese (grated)
- 1 cup reduced fat mozzarella cheese (shredded)
- 2 eggs
- 1 tbsp light butter
- 1 tbsp Worcestershire sauce
- 1 tsp dried thyme
- 1 tsp dried sage
- 1 tsp salt
- 1/2 tsp black pepper

Directions

- Prep Time 15 mins
- Cook Time 30 mins
- Total Time 45 mins
- Preheat oven to 400 degrees and spray a 2qt casserole dish with an olive oil mister or non-fat cooking spray.
- In a medium, nonstick skillet melt butter over medium high heat. Add in onions and celery, and cook until tender, about 5-7 minutes.
- Add in mushrooms, garlic, thyme, sage and salt and pepper, and cook until mushrooms are soft, about 5-7 minutes.
- Transfer mushroom mixture to a large bowl, and stir in all remaining ingredients, except for the shredded mozzarella.
- Pour into prepared casserole dish and top evenly with the shredded mozzarella.
- Place into oven and bake until cheese becomes golden and bubbly

Nutrition Information

Amount Per Serving

Calories 157 Calories from Fat 76

% Daily Value*

Total Fat 8.4g 13%

Saturated Fat 4.4g 22%

Cholesterol 73mg 24%

Sodium 657mg 27%

Potassium 311mg 9%

Total Carbohydrates 9.7g 3%

Dietary Fiber 1.7g 7%

Sugars 2.9g

Protein 13.5g 27%

Calcium 19%

Iron 16%

14

Shrimp Scampi

Ingredients

- 4 tsp olive oil
- 1 1/4 lb medium shrimp , peeled (tails left on)
- 6 to 8 garlic cloves, minced
- 1/2 cup low-sodium chicken broth
- 1/2 cup dry white wine
- 1/4 cup fresh lemon juice
- 1/4 cup plus 1 tablespoon fresh parsley, minced
- 1/4 tsp salt

- 1/4 tsp black pepper, freshly ground
- 4 slice lemon

Directions

- Prep 25 min
- Cook 0 min
- Ready 25 min
- In a large nonstick skillet, heat the oil. Sauté the shrimp until just pink, 2-3 minutes.
- Add the garlic and cook stirring constantly, about 30 seconds.
- With a slotted spoon transfer the shrimp to a platter, keep hot.
- In the skillet, combine the broth, wine, lemon juice, 1/4 cup of the parsley, the salt and pepper; bring to a boil.
- Boil, uncovered, until the sauce is reduced by half; spoon over the shrimp.
- Serve garnished with the lemon slices and sprinkled with the remaining tablespoon of parsley.
- Note: I have also added scallops to this with great results!

Nutritional Information

Serving Size: 1 (238 g)

Servings Per Recipe: 4

Amount Per Serving

Calories 184 Calories from Fat 56

% Daily Value

Total Fat 6g 9%

Saturated Fat 1g 4%

Cholesterol 179mg 59%

Sodium 964mg 40%

Total Carbohydrate 6g 2%

Dietary Fiber 1g 2%

Sugars 1g 3%

Protein 21g 41%

15
Hunan Shrimp

Ingredients

- 1 lb medium shrimp , peeled and deveined
- 1 tbsp corn starch
- 2 tsp corn starch
- 1/2 cup low-salt chicken broth
- 2 tbsp low-sodium soy sauce
- 1 tbsp black bean sauce
- 1 tbsp chili-garlic sauce

- 1 tbsp canola oil, divided
- 2 tbsp fresh ginger, peeled and minced
- 1 onion, cut into 1/4 inch slices
- 1 red bell pepper, seeded and cut into thin strips
- 1 green bell pepper, seeded and cut into thin strips
- 1/2 lb asparagus, trimmed and cut into 1 inch pieces
- 2 cup brown rice, cooked

Directions

- Prep 35 min
- Cook 10 min
- Ready 45 min
- Comine shrimp with 1 tablespoon cornstarch in a medium bowl; toss well to coat and set aside.
- Combine broth, soy sauce, black bean sauce, chili-garlic sauce, and 2 teaspoons cornstarch in a small bowl; set aside.
- Heat a nonstick wok or a large, deep skillet over medium-high heat until a drop of water sizzles.
- Swirl in 2 teaspoons oil, then add the shrimp.
- Stir-fry until just opaque in the center, about 3 minutes; transfer to a plate.
- Swirl in remaining 1 teaspoon oil, then add ginger and onion.
- Stir-fry until fragrant, about 1 miunte.
- Add bell peppers and asparagus; stir-fry until crisp-tender, about 2 minutes.
- Add shrimp and broth mixture.
- Cook, stirring constantly, until the mixture boils and thickens, about 1 minute.
- Serve over brown rice.

Nutritional Information

Serving Size: 1 (402 g)

Servings Per Recipe: 4

Amount Per Serving

Calories 284 Calories from Fat 53

% Daily Value

Total Fat 6g 9%

Saturated Fat 1g 3%

Cholesterol 143mg 47%

Sodium 932mg 38%

Total Carbohydrate 37g 12%

Dietary Fiber 5g 18%

Sugars 4g 16%

Protein 21g 42%

16

Baked Coconut Shrimp

Ingredients

- 2 large egg white
- 3/4 cup flour, divided
- 2/3 cup light beer
- 1 1/2 tsp baking powder
- 1/4 tsp salt
- 2 cup sweetened flaked coconut
- 24 large shrimp , peeled and deveined (with tails on)
- 1 nonstick cooking spray, 5 sprays (1 second each)

Directions

- Prep 20 min

- Cook 12 min
- Ready 32 min
- Preheat oven to 445 degrees F (230 degrees C).
- Spray a baking sheet with nonstick spray.
- In medium bowl, beat egg whites, 1/2 cup flour, beer, baking soda, and salt.
- Place remaining 1/4 cup of flour in a shallow dish and flaked coconut in another shallow dish.
- Pick up a shrimp by the tail and coat it well with flour.
- Next, dip the shrimp into the egg white mixture and then roll it in coconut.
- Press the coconut into the shrimp and place it on the prepared baking sheet.
- Repeat with each shrimp.
- Bake until the coconut is toasted and shrimp is done, about 10-12 minutes.

Nutritional Information

Serving Size: 1 (109 g)

Servings Per Recipe: 6

Amount Per Serving

Calories 256 Calories from Fat 104

% Daily Value

Total Fat 12g 17%

Saturated Fat 10g 49%

Cholesterol 43mg 14%

Sodium 330mg 13%

Total Carbohydrate 28g 9%

Dietary Fiber 2g 7%

Sugars 14g 54%

Protein 10g 18%

17

Creamy Shrimp with Angel Hair Pasta

Ingredients

- 6 oz angel hair pasta, uncooked
- 2 tbsp reduced-calorie margarine
- 1/4 cup scallion, sliced, about 3 large
- 3 tbsp fresh lemon juice, about 1 large lemon
- 2 large garlic cloves, minced
- 1 lb raw shrimp , peeled and deveined
- 1/2 cup fat-free half-and-half, or evaporated milk
- 1/4 cup tub-style light cream cheese
- 2 tbsp fresh dill weed, chopped, or 1 1/2 tsp dried dill

Directions

- Prep 20 min
- Cook 20 min
- Ready 40 min
- Cook pasta according to package directions, omitting salt and fat.
- Drain.
- While pasta cooks, melt margarine in a large nonstick skillet over medium-high heat.
- Add scallions, lemon juice, and garlic; cook for 2 minutes, stirring often.
- Add shrimp and cook for 5 minutes or until shrimp turn pink.
- Remove shrimp from skillet; set aside.
- Add half-and-half, cream cheese, and dill weed to the skillet, stirring until smooth.
- Cook for 1 to 2 minutes or until mixture is bubbly.

- Return shrimp to the skillet and cook until thoroughly heated.
- Combine shrimp mixture and pasta; toss well.

Nutritional Information

Serving Size: 1 (227 g)

Servings Per Recipe: 4

Amount Per Serving

Calories 332 Calories from Fat 81

% Daily Value

Total Fat 9g 13%

Saturated Fat 4g 17%

Cholesterol 160mg 53%

Sodium 780mg 32%

Total Carbohydrate 38g 12%

Dietary Fiber 2g 6%

Sugars 4g 14%

Protein 24g 46%

18

Spicy Baked Shrimp

Ingredients

- 2 tbsp lemon juice
- 1 tbsp honey
- 2 tsp dried parsley
- 2 tsp creole seasoning
- 1 tsp olive oil
- 2 tsp low-sodium soy sauce

- 1 lb large shrimp , peeled and deveined
- 1 olive oil-flavored cooking spray

Directions

- Prep 5 min
- Cook 8 min
- Ready 13 min
- Preheat oven to 450 degrees F (230 degrees C).
- Coat an 11 x 7 inch baking dish with cooking spray.
- Add lemon juice, honey, dried parsley, creole seasoning, olive oil, and soy sauce to dish and stir well to combine.
- Add shrimp and toss to coat.
- Bake for 8 minutes or until shrimp turn pink, stirring occasionally.

Nutritional Information

Serving Size: 1 (205 g)

Servings Per Recipe: 4

Amount Per Serving

Calories 111 Calories from Fat 20

% Daily Value

Total Fat 2g 3%

Saturated Fat 0g 1%

Cholesterol 143mg 47%

Sodium 813mg 33%

Total Carbohydrate 6g 2%

Dietary Fiber 0g

Sugars 5g 18%

Protein 16g 31%

19

Shrimp with Cilanto and Lime

Ingredients

- 1 3/4 lb large shrimp , peeled and deveined
- 2 tbsp fresh lime juice
- 1/2 tsp ground cumin
- 1/4 tsp ground ginger
- 2 garlic cloves, minced
- 1 tbsp olive oil
- 1/4 cup fresh cilantro, chopped
- 1 tsp lime, zest
- 1/2 tsp salt
- 1/4 tsp pepper

Directions

- Prep 15 min
- Cook 5 min
- Ready 20 min
- Combine shrimp, lime juice, cumin, ginger, and garlic in a large bowl; toss well.
- Heat oil in a large nonstick skillet over medium-high heat.
- Add shrimp mixture and saute for 4 minutes or until shrimp is done.
- Remove from heat; stir in cilantro, lime zest, salt, and pepper.

Nutritional Information

Serving Size: 1 (213 g)

Servings Per Recipe: 4

Amount Per Serving

Calories 177 Calories from Fat 49

% Daily Value

Total Fat 6g 8%

Saturated Fat 1g 3%

Cholesterol 251mg 83%

Sodium 1418mg 59%

Total Carbohydrate 3g 1%

Dietary Fiber 0g

Sugars 0g

Protein 27g 54%

20

Amazing Buffalo Chicken

Ingredients

- 1 lb boneless, skinless chicken breast
- 1/2 cup hot sauce
- 1/2 cup reduced-calorie vegetable oil-butter spread
- 1/4 tsp celery seeds
- 1 tbsp white vinegar
- 1/2 tsp tabasco sauce
- 1/2 tsp red pepper flakes
- 1/4 tsp black pepper
- 1/2 tsp cayenne pepper
- 1/4 tsp Worcestershire sauce

Directions

- Prep 15 min
- Cook 15 min

- Ready 30 min
- For the sauce: In a small saucepan over low heat, mix together everything except the chicken. Simmer, stirring occasionally, while you prepare chicken.
- For the chicken: Bring water to a boil in a large saucepan. Cut chicken into strips and boil until cooked through. When cooked, put chicken in a serving bowl or dish. Pour sauce over chicken and let it sit for a few minutes.
- Variation: Cut chicken into strips. Lightly coat chicken with sauce. Bake in a preheated 375 degree F (190 degrees C) oven for 15-20 minutes until cooked through. Remove to a platter and coat with remaining sauce.

Nutritional Information

Serving Size: 1 (117 g)

Servings Per Recipe: 4

Amount Per Serving

Calories 136   Calories from Fat 28

% Daily Value

Total Fat 3g 4%

Saturated Fat 1g 3%

Cholesterol 73mg 24%

Sodium 885mg 36%

Total Carbohydrate 1g

Dietary Fiber 0g 1%

Sugars 0g 1%

Protein 24g 48%

Parmesan Chicken with Mushroom Wine Sauce

Ingredients

- 2 tbsp flour
- 2 tbsp parmesan cheese, grated
- 1/2 tsp salt, divided
- 1/4 tsp pepper
- 16 oz chicken breast
- 1 tbsp olive oil, divided
- 2 cup onion, diced
- 2 garlic cloves, minced
- 2 cup mushrooms, sliced
- 1/2 tsp basil
- 2 tbsp dry white wine
- 2 tbsp water

Directions

- Prep 15 min
- Cook 20 min
- Ready 35 min
- On a sheet of wax paper or paper plate, combine flour, parmesan cheese, and 1/4 tsp each salt and pepper.
- Dredge chicken in flour mixture, coating both sides, and reserve any remaining flour mixture.
- In a 10 inch skillet, heat 1 1/2 tsps oil over medium-high heat; add onions and garlic and saute until onions are softened.
- Add mushrooms, basil, and remaining 1/4 tsp salt and saute until mushrooms are tender, about 5 minutes.
- Transfer mixture to plate and set aside.
- In the same skillet, heat remaining 1 1/2 tsp oil; add chicken and cook, turning once, until lightly browned, 1 to 2 minutes on each side.

- Stir in reserved flour mixture; gradually add wine and water and continuing to stir, bring mixture to a boil.
- Return mushroom mixture to the pan and cook until heated through.

Nutritional Information

Serving Size: 1 (255 g)

Servings Per Recipe: 4

Amount Per Serving

Calories 298 Calories from Fat 133

% Daily Value

Total Fat 15g 22%

Saturated Fat 4g 19%

Cholesterol 75mg 24%

Sodium 406mg 16%

Total Carbohydrate 13g 4%

Dietary Fiber 2g 7%

Sugars 4g 16%

Protein 27g 54%

22

Beef Stroganoff

Ingredients

- 6 oz lean sirloin steak
- 1 1/2 cup fresh mushrooms, sliced
- 1/2 cup onion, sliced

- 3 garlic cloves, minced
- 1/2 cup beef broth
- 1/4 cup tomato sauce
- 3 tbsp dry sherry, optional
- 3/4 tsp Worcestershire sauce
- 1/4 tsp salt
- 1/4 tsp black pepper
- 1/3 cup fat-free sour cream
- 1 cup dry medium egg noodles, cooked
- 2 tsp fresh parsley, chopped

Directions

- Prep 15 min
- Cook 60 min
- Ready 75 min
- Trim fat from steak.
- Slice steak diagonally across grain into 1/4 inch wide strips.
- Place a non-stick skillet over medium high heat until hot.
- Add steak; cook 3 minutes.
- Drain well.
- Place skillet over medium-high heat until hot.
- Return steak to skillet.
- Add mushrooms, onion, and garlic; saute 2 minutes.
- Add beef broth and next 5 ingredients; bring to boil.
- Cover, reduce heat, and simmer 50 minutes or until meat is tender.
- Remove from heat; stir in sour cream. Spoon over noodles; sprinkle with parsley.

Nutritional Information

Serving Size: 1 (426 g)

Servings Per Recipe: 2

Amount Per Serving

Calories 198 Calories from Fat 23

% Daily Value

Total Fat 3g 4%

Saturated Fat 1g 4%

Cholesterol 27mg 9%

Sodium 736mg 30%

Total Carbohydrate 36g 11%

Dietary Fiber 3g 11%

Sugars 8g 30%

Protein 9g 18%

23

Skinny Sweet and Sour Pork

Ingredients

- 1 lb pork tenderloin, trimmed of all visible fat and cut into 1/2 inch cubes
- 2 tbsp corn starch, divided
- 1/3 cup water
- 1/4 cup rice vinegar
- 1/4 cup white sugar
- 3 tbsp ketchup
- 2 tbsp low-sodium soy sauce
- 1 tbsp canola oil
- 1 tbsp fresh ginger, peeled and minced
- 2 clove garlic, minced
- 1 bell pepper, seeded and cut into 1/2 inch pieces

- 1 can (8 oz) pineapple chunks, juice drained

Directions

- Prep 15 min
- Cook 15 min
- Ready 30 min
- Combine pork with 1 tablespoon corn starch in a medium bowl; toss well to coat and set aside. Combine remaining 1 tablespoon corn starch, water, vinegar, sugar, ketchup, and soy sauce in a small bowl; set aside.
- Heat a nonstick wok or a large, deep skillet over medium-high heat until a drop of water sizzles. Swirl in the oil, then add the pork; stir-fry until almost cooked through, 2-3 minutes. Add ginger and garlic; stir-fry until fragrant, about 30 seconds. Add bell pepper and pineapple; stir-fry until crisp-tender, about 3 minutes. Add the vinegar mixture and cook, stirring constantly, until the mixture boils and thickens and the pork is just cooked through, 1-2 minutes.

Nutritional Information

Serving Size: 1 (268 g)

Servings Per Recipe: 4

Amount Per Serving

Calories 289   Calories from Fat 68

% Daily Value

Total Fat 8g 11%

Saturated Fat 2g 8%

Cholesterol 74mg 24%

Sodium 454mg 18%

Total Carbohydrate 31g 10%

Dietary Fiber 1g 4%

Sugars 24g 96%

Protein 25g 49%

24

Crustless Spinach and Mushroom Quiche

Ingredients

- 10 oz frozen spinach
- 1 cup mushrooms, sliced
- 1 cup artichoke hearts, chopped
- 1/2 tsp olive oil
- 1/2 cup fat-free cottage cheese
- 2 tsp garlic, minced
- 1/2 medium onion, chopped
- 3 egg
- 1 salt
- 1 black pepper
- 1 nonstick cooking spray

Directions

- Prep 5 min
- Cook 60 min
- Ready 65 min
- Preheat oven to 350 degrees.
- Saute mushrooms and onions in olive oil with garlic. Add spinach and cook until liquid has reduced.
- Mix vegetables with remaining ingredients, salt and pepper to taste.
- Pour into pie dish sprayed with nonstick spray. Bake 45 minutes.

Nutritional Information
Serving Size: 1 (208 g)
Servings Per Recipe: 4
Amount Per Serving
Calories 128 Calories from Fat 43
% Daily Value
Total Fat 5g 7%
Saturated Fat 1g 6%
Cholesterol 141mg 46%
Sodium 198mg 8%
Total Carbohydrate 12g 4%
Dietary Fiber 6g 25%
Sugars 2g 9%
Protein 11g 22%

25

Stuffed Baked Potatoes

Ingredients

- 2 large baking potato
- 2 tsp olive oil
- 2 onion, chopped
- 1 cup broccoli, chopped
- 1 cup carrot, chopped
- 4 garlic cloves, minced
- 1/2 cup non-fat cottage cheese
- 1/4 cup parsley, chopped
- 2 tbsp parmesan cheese, grated
- 1/2 tsp ground black pepper
- 1/4 tsp salt

Directions

- Prep 15 min
- Cook 90 min
- Ready 105 min
- Preheat oven to 400 degrees F (200 degrees C).
- Poke potatoes with a fork. Bake for 1 hour.
- While potatoes are baking, heat oil in a medium skillet. Saute onions for about 5 minutes.
- Add broccoli, carrot, and garlic and stir until softened, about 5 minutes. Reduce heat, cover, and cook for 4 minutes longer.
- When potatoes are done, remove from the oven and reduce temperature to 350 degrees F (175 degrees C).
- Cut potatoes in half and scoop out pulp into a large bowl. Set skins aside.
- Add sauteed vegetables, cottage cheese, parsley, parmesan cheese, salt, and pepper to potato pulp. Mash up well.
- Spoon mixture into potato skins.
- Place stuffed potatoes on a baking sheet and bake until heated through for 15 minutes.

Nutritional Information

Serving Size: 1 (214 g)

Servings Per Recipe: 4

Amount Per Serving

Calories 158   Calories from Fat 30

% Daily Value

Total Fat 3g 5%

Saturated Fat 1g 4%

Cholesterol 4mg 1%

Sodium 281mg 11%

Total Carbohydrate 28g 9%

Dietary Fiber 4g 16%

Sugars 5g 21%

Protein 6g 12%

26

Slow Cooker Tomato Spinach Soup

Ingredients

- 10 oz baby spinach, washed
- 2 medium carrots, chopped
- 2 medium stalks celery, chopped
- 1 large onion, chopped
- 1 clove garlic, minced
- 4 cup low sodium vegetable broth
- 1 can (28 oz) diced tomatoes
- 2 bay leaves
- 1 tbsp dried basil

- 1 tsp dried oregano
- 1/2 tsp crushed red pepper flakes

Directions

- Prep 5 min
- Cook 600 min
- Ready 605 min
- Place all ingredients in a slow cooker.
- Cover and cook on High for 5 hours or Low for 8-10 hours.
- Remove bay leaves, stir, and serve.

Nutritional Information

Serving Size: 1 (179 g)

Servings Per Recipe: 8

Amount Per Serving

Calories 43 Calories from Fat 4

% Daily Value

Total Fat 0g

Saturated Fat 0g

Cholesterol 0mg

Sodium 53mg 2%

Total Carbohydrate 9g 3%

Dietary Fiber 3g 12%

Sugars 5g 17%

Protein 2g 4%

Deep Dish Pizza Casserole

Ingredients

- 1 lb ground round
- 1 can (15 oz) chunky Italian style tomatoes
- 1 can (10 oz) refrigerated pizza dough
- 6 oz part-skim mozzarella cheese, shredded
- 1 cooking spray

Directions

- Prep 15 min
- Cook 17 min
- Ready 32 min
- Preheat oven to 425 degrees F (220 degrees C).
- Cook meat in a nonstick skillet over medium-high heat until browned, stirring until it crumbles. Drain, if necessary, and return to skillet. Add tomatoes and cook until heated through.
- While meat cooks, coat a 13 x 9 inch baking dish with cooking spray. Unroll pizza crust dough and press into bottom and halfway up sides of the baking dish. Top the pizza crust with meat mixture.
- Bake uncovered for 12 minutes. Top with cheese and bake another 5 minutes or until crust is browned and cheese melts.
- Cool 5 minutes before serving.

Nutritional Information

Serving Size: 1 (174 g)

Servings Per Recipe: 6

Amount Per Serving

Calories 283 Calories from Fat 177

% Daily Value

Total Fat 20g 30%

Saturated Fat 9g 43%

Cholesterol 72mg 23%

Sodium 383mg 15%

Total Carbohydrate 5g 1%

Dietary Fiber 1g 2%

Sugars 3g 11%

Protein 21g 41%

28

Copycat Applebee's Low Fat Veggie Quesadilla

Ingredients

- 1/2 tbsp canola oil
- 1/2 cup mushrooms, sliced
- 1/3 cup carrot, shredded
- 1/3 cup broccoli, chopped
- 2 tbsp onion, diced
- 1 tbsp red bell pepper, diced
- 1 tsp soy sauce
- 1 dash cayenne pepper
- 1 dash black pepper
- 1 dash salt
- 2 wheat flour tortilla
- 1/4 cup fat-free cheddar cheese, shredded

- 1/4 cup fat-free mozzarella cheese, shredded
- 1 nonstick cooking spray

Directions

- Prep 10 min
- Cook 5 min
- Ready 15 min
- In a frying pan that has a bigger diameter than the tortillas, saute the vegetables in the oil over medium/high heat for 5 to 7 minutes. Season with soy sauce, peppers, and salt.
- Pour the vegetables into a bowl, and place the frying pan back on the heat to medium/low.
- Place one of the tortillas in the pan, and sprinkle half of the cheeses on the tortilla. Spread the vegetables over the cheese, then sprinkle the rest of the cheeses over the vegetables. Put the second tortilla on top and cook for 1 to 2 minutes, or until heated through and the cheese is melted. Flip quesadilla over and cook 1-2 min more.
- Slide the quesadilla onto cutting board and slice it like a pizza into 6 equal pieces. Serve hot with fat-free sour cream, salsa, and shredded lettuce on the side.

Nutritional Information

Serving Size: 1 (81 g)

Servings Per Recipe: 2

Amount Per Serving

Calories 76 Calories from Fat 33

% Daily Value

Total Fat 4g 5%

Saturated Fat 0g 1%

Cholesterol 3mg

Sodium 371mg 15%

Total Carbohydrate 6g 1%

Dietary Fiber 2g 7%

Sugars 2g 8%

Protein 6g 12%

29

Egg Salad

Ingredients

- 4 large egg
- 2 large egg white, boil as whole eggs and discard the yolks
- 2 tbsp fresh chives, chopped
- 2 tbsp reduced-calorie mayonnaise
- 1/2 tsp dijon mustard
- 1/2 tsp table salt
- 1 dill
- 1/4 tsp black pepper, freshly ground

Directions

- Prep 10 min
- Cook 10 min
- Ready 20 min
- Place eggs in a medium saucepan and pour in enough water to cover them; set pan over high heat and bring to a boil.
- Boil 10 minutes; drain and place eggs in an ice-water bath.
- When eggs are cool enough to handle, remove shells.
- Discard yolks from two of the eggs. Cut remaining whole eggs and whites into 1/2-inch pieces (or use an egg slicer).
- Transfer eggs to a medium bowl. Add chives, mayonnaise, mustard, dill, salt and pepper; mix until blended.

Nutritional Information

Serving Size: 1 (77 g)

Servings Per Recipe: 4

Amount Per Serving

Calories 106 Calories from Fat 65

% Daily Value

Total Fat 7g 11%

Saturated Fat 2g 9%

Cholesterol 189mg 62%

Sodium 456mg 19%

Total Carbohydrate 1g

Dietary Fiber 0g

Sugars 1g 2%

Protein 8g 16%

30

Turkey Sausage and Bell Peppers

Ingredients

- 1/4 lb Italian turkey sausage, cut into 1/4 in. slices
- 1 red bell pepper, sliced
- 1 green bell pepper, sliced
- 1 yellow bell pepper, sliced
- 1 onion, sliced
- 1/4 cup chicken broth
- 2 tbsp garlic, minced
- 1/4 tsp crushed red pepper flakes

- 1/4 tsp dried oregano, leaves

Directions

- Prep 15 min
- Cook 10 min
- Ready 25 min
- Spray large skillet with Pam cooking spray and heat skillet.
- Add sausage and stir frequently until no longer pink 5-6 minutes.
- Add bell peppers, onion, broth, garlic, pepper flakes and oregano. Saute all together for 5 minutes or until liquid evaporates.
- Reduce heat and simmer covered 5 minutes more.

Nutritional Information

Serving Size: 1 (181 g)

Servings Per Recipe: 4

Amount Per Serving

Calories 93   Calories from Fat 25

% Daily Value

Total Fat 3g 4%

Saturated Fat 0g

Cholesterol 15mg 5%

Sodium 315mg 13%

Total Carbohydrate 12g 3%

Dietary Fiber 2g 9%

Sugars 4g 16%

Protein 6g 12%

CHAPTER FIVE
30 RECIPES FOR LAUNCH
LUNCH: 01

Juicy Hamburgers

Ingredients

- 1 cooking spray
- 1 lb uncooked 93% lean ground beef
- 1 tbsp Worcestershire sauce
- 2 tsp garlic, minced
- 1/2 tsp table salt
- 1/4 tsp black pepper, freshly ground
- 4 reduced-calorie hamburger buns

Directions

- Prep 8 min
- Cook 10 min
- Ready 18 min
- Coat a large griddle, outdoor grill rack or stovetop grill pan with cooking spray and preheat to medium-high.
- In a large bowl, combine beef, Worcestershire sauce, garlic, salt and pepper. Mix well and shape mixture into 4 patties, about 1-inch thick each.
- Place burgers on hot griddle or grill and cook 5 minutes per side for medium (or longer until desired doneness).
- Serve burgers on buns with your favorite 0 POINTS value toppings.

Nutritional Information

Serving Size: 1 (120 g)

Servings Per Recipe: 4

Amount Per Serving

Calories 161 Calories from Fat 51

% Daily Value

Total Fat 6g 8%

Saturated Fat 3g 12%

Cholesterol 70mg 23%

Sodium 407mg 16%

Total Carbohydrate 1g

Dietary Fiber 0g

Sugars 0g 1%

Protein 24g 48%

LUNCH: 02

Shrimp & Broccoli in Chili Sauce

Ingredients

- 1 1/2 lb medium shrimp , peeled and deveined
- 2 tbsp jalapeno pepper, minced, seeded (about 2 peppers)
- 2 tbsp dry sherry
- 1 1/2 tsp paprika
- 1/2 tsp ground red pepper
- 4 clove garlic, crushed
- 1/3 cup water
- 1/4 cup chili sauce, such as Heinz
- 2 tsp corn starch
- 2 tsp sugar
- 1/2 tsp salt
- 1 tbsp oil

- 3 cup broccoli, cut into florets
- 4 cup cooked soba noodles, about 8 oz uncooked buckwheat noodles, or vermicelli

Directions

- Prep 75 min
- Cook 20 min
- Ready 95 min
- Combine the first 6 ingredients in a medium bowl, cover and chill for 1 hour. Combine water and next 5 ingredients (water through salt) in a bowl, set aside. Heat oil in a stir fry pan or wok over medium-high heat.
- add broccoli, stir fry 2 minutes.
- add shrimp mixture, stir fry 5 minutes or until shrimp are done.
- Add cornstarch mixture and bring to a boil.
- cook 1 minute or until sauce thickens.
- serve over soba noodles.

LUNCH: 03
Crab Quesadillas

Ingredients

- 8 oz imitation crabmeat
- 1/2 cup monterey jack cheese, or cheddar cheese, shredded
- 1 can (4 ounce) diced green chiles
- 1/4 cup tomato, chopped
- 2 tbsp green bell pepper, chopped
- 4 (8 inch) tortillas

Directions

- Prep 5 min
- Cook 15 min
- Ready 20 min
- Preheat oven to 425 degrees F (220 degrees C).

- In a bowl, mix crabmeat, cheese, chilies, tomatoes, and bell peppers.
- Spray one side of a tortilla with nonstick cooking spray.
- Turn the tortilla over, spoon 1/4 of the crab mixture onto the unsprayed side, and fold in half.
- Place quesadilla on a baking sheet. Repeat with remaining ingredients.
- Bake uncovered for 10 minutes, then turn over and bake for an additional 5 minutes or until the cheese is melted.

Nutritional Information

Serving Size: 1 (171 g)

Servings Per Recipe: 4

Amount Per Serving

Calories 290 Calories from Fat 80

% Daily Value

Total Fat 9g 13%

Saturated Fat 4g 19%

Cholesterol 24mg 7%

Sodium 1244mg 51%

Total Carbohydrate 39g 13%

Dietary Fiber 3g 10%

Sugars 6g 23%

Protein 13g 25%

LUNCH: 04
Italian Tuna Salad Sandwich

Ingredients

- 4 cup lettuce, shredded
- 8 oz solid white tuna in water, drained and flaked
- 1 medium red onion, very thinly sliced
- 1 tbsp capers, rinsed and drained
- 3 tbsp balsamic vinegar
- 1 tbsp olive oil, plus 1 tsp
- 1 clove garlic, minced
- 1 tsp dried oregano
- 1/2 tsp black pepper, freshly ground
- 1/4 tsp salt
- 1 loaf (8 ounce) Italian bread
- 2 medium tomatoes, sliced

Directions

- Prep 15 min
- Cook 0 min
- Ready 15 min
- To make the tuna salad: In medium bowl, combine lettuce, tuna, onion and capers; set aside.
- To make the dressing: In small jar with a tight-fitting lid or small bowl, combine vinegar, olive oil, garlic, oregano, pepper and salt; cover and shake well or blend until combined with a wire whisk.
- Pour dressing over salad; toss to combine.
- To make the sandwiches: Split bread lengthwise almost all the way through; spread open.
- Line the bottom half of the bread with tomatoes; top evenly with the salad mixture.
- Replace top half of the bread to enclose.
- Wrap tightly in plastic wrap; refrigerate for 2 hours until chilled and the flavors are blended.
- Cut loaf crosswise through the plastic wrap into 4 equal portions.

Nutritional Information

Serving Size: 1 (277 g)

Servings Per Recipe: 4

Amount Per Serving

Calories 389 Calories from Fat 107

% Daily Value

Total Fat 12g 18%

Saturated Fat 2g 10%

Cholesterol 18mg 5%

Sodium 889mg 37%

Total Carbohydrate 46g 15%

Dietary Fiber 4g 15%

Sugars 6g 22%

Protein 23g 46%

LUNCH: 05

Low Fat Chicken Fried Steak

Ingredients

- 4 piece lean cube steak
- 1/2 cup fat-free buttermilk
- 1 cup flour, reserve 1 tbsp
- 1 tsp salt
- 1 tsp steak seasoning, such as McCormick Montreal Steak
- 2 tbsp oil
- 2 cup skim milk

Directions

- Prep 30 min
- Cook 10 min
- Ready 40 min
- Dip steaks in buttermilk. Combine flour, salt, and steak seasoning (remember to keep 1 tablespoon set aside). Dip steaks in flour mixture.
- Set steaks on wax paper, let set for 20 minutes.
- Heat 1 tablespoons oil in skillet, add steaks, cook until both sides are golden brown. Remove from pan and keep warm.

- Combine milk and reserved tablespoon of flour in bowl until well mixed.
- Stirring constantly, add milk mixture to skillet. Once added, bring mixture to a boil.
- Lower heat and simmer until gravy thickens. Serve over steaks.

Nutritional Information

Serving Size: 1 (162 g)

Servings Per Recipe: 4

Amount Per Serving

Calories 224 Calories from Fat 66

% Daily Value

Total Fat 7g 11%

Saturated Fat 1g 5%

Cholesterol 3mg

Sodium 655mg 27%

Total Carbohydrate 31g 10%

Dietary Fiber 1g 3%

Sugars 0g

Protein 8g 16%

LUNCH: 06

Homemade Salisbury Steak

Ingredients

- 1 lb ground round

- 2/3 cup onion, finely chopped
- 1/3 cup instant rice
- 1/4 tsp black pepper
- 1/8 tsp salt
- 1 large egg white
- 1 cooking spray
- 1 1/4 cup fresh mushrooms, sliced
- 2 can (10 1/2 oz each) beef consomme
- 1 1/2 tbsp Worcestershire sauce
- 2 tbsp water
- 1 1/2 tbsp corn starch

Directions

- Prep 15 min
- Cook 45 min
- Ready 60 min
- Combine ground round, onion, rice, pepper, salt, and egg white in a bowl; stir well.
- Divide mixture into 4 equal portions, shaping each into a 1/2-inch-thick patty.
- Coat a large nonstick skillet with cooking spray; place over medium-high heat until hot.
- Add patties, and cook 5 minutes on each side or until browned.
- Remove patties from skillet; set aside, and keep warm.
- Recoat skillet with cooking spray.
- Add mushrooms; saute' over medium-high heat 3 minutes.
- Add consomme' and Worcestershire sauce; cook 10 minutes.
- Return patties to skillet.
- Cover; reduce heat; and simmer 15 minutes.
- Remove patties from skillet; set aside, and keep warm.

- Combine water and cornstarch; stir well.
- Stir cornstarch mixture into broth mixture in skillet; bring to a boil, and cook 1 minute or until thick, stirring constantly.
- Spoon gravy over patties.

Nutritional Information

Serving Size: 1 (344 g)

Servings Per Recipe: 4

Amount Per Serving

Calories 374 Calories from Fat 205

% Daily Value

Total Fat 23g 35%

Saturated Fat 9g 43%

Cholesterol 81mg 26%

Sodium 1200mg 50%

Total Carbohydrate 15g 5%

Dietary Fiber 1g 3%

Sugars 2g 9%

Protein 26g 51%

LUNCH: 07

Loaded Baked Potato Soup

Ingredients

- 1 large bulb garlic, 1/4-inch-slice cut off top

- 3 lb potato, rinsed, pierced with a fork (about 6 large baking potatoes)
- 6 slice uncooked turkey bacon
- 4 cup reduced-sodium chicken broth
- 1 1/2 tbsp fresh thyme, chopped
- 1/2 tsp salt
- 1/4 tsp black pepper, freshly ground
- 6 tbsp reduced-fat sour cream
- 6 tbsp low-fat cheddar cheese, shredded
- 6 tbsp scallion, sliced

Directions

- Prep 15 min
- Cook 70 min
- Ready 85 min
- Preheat oven to 400°F.
- Wrap entire garlic bulb tightly in foil; place garlic and potatoes in oven. (You do not need to put them on a pan; they can go right on an oven rack.).
- Bake garlic until soft when squeezed, about 45 minutes; remove from oven and let cool. Continue baking potatoes until tender when pierced, about 15 minutes more; let potatoes stand until cool enough to handle.
- Meanwhile, cook bacon in a large nonstick skillet over medium-high heat until browned, about 6 minutes.
- Place bacon on paper towels to drain off any fat; chop bacon.
- Unwrap garlic and squeeze pulp from bulb with hands into a large saucepan.
- Peel potatoes and add to saucepan; mash with a potato masher until smooth.
- Gradually stir in broth, thyme, salt and pepper until blended; place saucepan over medium heat and cook until hot, stirring occasionally, about 5 to 10 minutes.
- Spoon about 1 1/3 cups of soup into each of 6 soup bowls.

- Top each with 1 tablespoon of sour cream, 1 tablespoon of cheese, 1 rounded tablespoon of bacon and 1 tablespoon of scallions.
- Grind fresh pepper over top if desired.

Nutritional Information

Serving Size: 1 (430 g)

Servings Per Recipe: 6

Amount Per Serving

Calories 271 Calories from Fat 56

% Daily Value

Total Fat 6g 9%

Saturated Fat 3g 12%

Cholesterol 20mg 6%

Sodium 476mg 19%

Total Carbohydrate 43g 14%

Dietary Fiber 5g 21%

Sugars 2g 9%

Protein 12g 24%

LUNCH: 08

Easy Barbecue Chicken

- Ingredients
- 1/2 cup ketchup
- 2 tbsp onion, finely chopped
- 2 tbsp peach or apricot preserves

- 2 tbsp white vinegar
- 1 tsp Worcestershire sauce
- 1 1/2 tsp chili powder
- 1/8 tsp garlic powder
- 1 cooking spray
- 6 oz chicken breast, halves (bone-in)

Directions

- Prep 10 min
- Cook 20 min
- Ready 30 min
- Combine ketchup, onions, jam, vinegar, Worcestershire sauce, chili powder and garlic powder in a small saucepan; bring to a boil.
- Reduce heat, and simmer, uncovered, 5 minutes.
- Set aside 1/2 cup sauce; keep warm.
- Coat grill rack with cooking spray; place on grill over medium-hot coals (350 to 400 degrees).
- Place chicken, bone side up, on rack; grill, covered, 8 minutes on each side or until done, turning once and basting with remaining barbecue sauce.
- Serve with reserved 1/2 cup barbecue sauce.

Nutritional Information

Serving Size: 1 (226 g)

Servings Per Recipe: 4

Amount Per Serving

Calories 260 Calories from Fat 42

% Daily Value

Total Fat 5g 7%

Saturated Fat 1g 5%

Cholesterol 110mg 36%

Sodium 567mg 23%

Total Carbohydrate 16g 5%

Dietary Fiber 1g 2%

Sugars 12g 48%

Protein 37g 74%

LUNCH: 09

Shepherd's Pie

Ingredients

- 2 large potato, peeled and cut into 2-inch pieces
- 1/4 cup non-fat sour cream
- 1 tbsp reduced-calorie margarine
- 1/8 tsp table salt
- 2 tsp olive oil
- 1 cup onion, chopped
- 2 medium carrot, diced
- 2 medium ribs celery, diced
- 1 lb uncooked ground turkey breast
- 3 tbsp all-purpose flour
- 1 tbsp fresh rosemary, chopped, or 1 teaspoon dried rosemary
- 1 tsp dried thyme
- 1/2 tsp salt
- 1/4 tsp black pepper
- 2 cup canned chicken broth, or beef broth

Directions

- Prep 25 min
- Cook 42 min

- Ready 67 min
- Preheat oven to 400°F.
- Place potatoes in a large saucepan and pour in enough water to cover potatoes. Set pan over high heat and bring to a boil; reduce heat to medium and simmer 10 minutes, until potatoes are fork-tender. Drain potatoes, transfer to a large bowl and add sour cream and margarine; mash until smooth, season to taste with salt and set aside.
- Meanwhile, heat oil in a large skillet over medium-high heat. Add onion, carrots and celery; cook until soft, about 3 minutes. Add turkey and cook until browned, breaking up the meat as it cooks, about 5 minutes. Add flour, rosemary, thyme, salt and pepper; stir to coat. Add broth and bring to a simmer; simmer until mixture thickens, about 3 minutes.
- Transfer turkey mixture to a 9-inch, deep-dish pie plate. Spread mashed potatoes over top and using the back of a spoon, make decorative swirls over the top. Bake until potatoes are golden, about 30 minutes. Slice into 6 pieces and serve.

Nutritional Information

Serving Size: 1 (362 g)

Servings Per Recipe: 6

Amount Per Serving

Calories 274 Calories from Fat 40

% Daily Value

Total Fat 4g 6%

Saturated Fat 1g 5%

Cholesterol 50mg 16%

Sodium 856mg 35%

Total Carbohydrate 32g 10%

Dietary Fiber 4g 16%

Sugars 4g 17%

Protein 26g 52%

LUNCH: 10

Potato Salad with Bacon

Ingredients

- 1 1/2 lb red potato, uncooked
- 3 slice turkey bacon
- 1/2 cup scallion, chopped
- 1/4 cup reduced calorie mayonnaise
- 2 tbsp red wine vinegar
- 2 tbsp fresh parsley, chopped
- 1/2 tsp table salt
- 1/4 tsp black pepper, freshly ground

Directions

- Prep 10 min
- Cook 20 min
- Ready 30 min
* Place potatoes in a large saucepan and pour in enough water to cover them; set pan over high heat and bring to a boil. Reduce heat to medium and simmer until potatoes are fork-tender, about 20 minutes; drain. When potatoes are cool enough to handle, slice each into quarters.
* Meanwhile, cook bacon in a hot skillet or in the microwave until crisp; drain on paper towels. Break bacon into small pieces.
* Transfer potatoes to a large bowl; add bacon and scallions. Add mayonnaise, vinegar, parsley, salt, and pepper; mix until blended.

Nutritional Information

Serving Size: 1 (218 g)

Servings Per Recipe: 4

Amount Per Serving

Calories 204 Calories from Fat 66

% Daily Value

Total Fat 7g 11%

Saturated Fat 1g 6%

Cholesterol 15mg 4%

Sodium 551mg 22%

Total Carbohydrate 30g 9%

Dietary Fiber 3g 13%

Sugars 3g 11%

Protein 5g 10%

LUNCH: 11

Broccoli Quiche

Ingredients

3/4 cup liquid egg substitute

1 1/2 cup 1% low-fat milk

3/4 cup low-fat baking mix, such as Bisquick

1 tsp salt

1/4 tsp black pepper, ground

2 garlic cloves, chopped

20 oz chopped frozen broccoli, or spinach

1 medium onion, chopped

1 red bell pepper, chopped

4 oz part-skim mozzarella cheese

Directions

- Prep 10 min
- Cook 45 min
- Ready 55 min
- Thaw, rinse, and drain broccoli.
- Put 1/2 of broccoli in 11 x 7 glass pan sprayed with cooking spray.
- Put 1/2 onion, 1/2 bell pepper and all of cheese on top of that.

- Put remaining broccoli, onion and bell pepper on top of that.
- Blend egg substitute, milk, biscuit mix, salt, black pepper, and garlic in a blender until smooth.
- Pour mixture over broccoli in pan.
- Bake at 400 degrees for 50 minutes or until lightly browned. Cut into 6 pieces when cool.

Nutritional Information

Serving Size: 1 (215 g)

Servings Per Recipe: 6

Amount Per Serving

Calories 114 Calories from Fat 35

% Daily Value

Total Fat 4g 6%

Saturated Fat 2g 11%

Cholesterol 15mg 5%

Sodium 556mg 23%

Total Carbohydrate 11g 3%

Dietary Fiber 4g 14%

Sugars 6g 25%

Protein 10g 19%

LUNCH: 12

Crock Pot Teriyaki Chicken

Ingredients

- 2 1/2 lb boneless, skinless chicken breast, cut into 2 inch pieces
- 1/2 cup soy sauce
- 1/2 cup honey
- 3 whole garlic cloves
- 1 hot chili sauce, optional

Directions

- Prep 5 min
- Cook 240 min
- Ready 245 min
- Add chicken to a crock pot with soy sauce, honey, garlic cloves and hot chili sauce, if using.
- Set the crock pot to Low and cover.
- Stir after 2 hours and then cook an additional 2 hours.
- Remove garlic cloves.

Nutritional Information

Serving Size: 1 (243 g)

Servings Per Recipe: 6

Amount Per Serving

Calories 318 Calories from Fat 44

% Daily Value

Total Fat 5g 7%

Saturated Fat 1g 5%

Cholesterol 121mg 40%

Sodium 1562mg 65%

Total Carbohydrate 25g 8%

Dietary Fiber 0g 1%

Sugars 24g 94%

Protein 43g 85%

LUNCH: 13

Italian Chicken Cacciatore

Ingredients

- 1 tbsp (up to 2) olive oil
- 2 bell pepper, chopped
- 2 onion, chopped
- 1 clove (up to 2) garlic, chopped (optional)
- 2 whole boneless, skinless chicken breast, cut into bite sized pieces
- 1 can (14 1/2 oz) diced tomatoes
- 1 can (6 oz) tomato paste
- 6 oz water
- 2 package (1 g each) Splenda sugar substitute, or to taste
- 1 dash red pepper flakes
- 1 tsp basil
- 1 tsp oregano
- 1 lb whole-wheat spaghetti

Directions

- Prep 15 min
- Cook 45 min
- Ready 60 min
- Preheat oven to 400 degrees F (205 degrees C).
- Add olive oil, bell peppers, onions, garlic (if using), chicken, diced tomatoes, tomato paste, water, Splenda sugar substitute, red pepper flakes, basil, and oregano to a baking dish, stir to combine, and cover.

- Bake for 45 minutes. Uncover and stir. Return to the oven and continue baking until the chicken is cooked through and the vegetables are desired doneness.
- Meanwhile, bring a large pot of lightly salted water to a boil. Cook pasta according to the package directions, then drain.
- Serve chicken and sauce over the pasta.

Nutritional Information

Serving Size: 1 (376 g)

Servings Per Recipe: 4

Amount Per Serving

Calories 730   Calories from Fat 116

% Daily Value

Total Fat 13g 19%

Saturated Fat 2g 11%

Cholesterol 76mg 25%

Sodium 503mg 20%

Total Carbohydrate 120g 40%

Dietary Fiber 12g 47%

Sugars 15g 58%

Protein 49g 97%

LUNCH: 14

Skinny Chimichangas

Ingredients

- 1/2 lb ground turkey breast
- 1 onion, finely chopped
- 1 clove garlic, minced
- 2 tsp chili powder
- 1 tsp dried oregano
- 1/2 tsp ground cumin
- 1 can (8 oz) tomato sauce
- 2 tbsp mild green chili pepper, chopped
- 1/3 cup reduced-fat cheddar cheese, shredded
- 4 (8 inch each) fat-free flour tortillas

Directions

- Prep 15 min
- Cook 40 min
- Ready 55 min
- Preheat the oven to 400 degrees F.
- Spray a nonstick baking sheet with nonstick spray; set aside.
- Spray a medium nonstick skillet with nonstick spray; set over medium-high heat.
- Add the turkey, onion, garlic, chili powder, oregano, and cumin.
- Cook, breaking up the turkey with a wooden spoon until browned, about 6 miuntes.
- Stir in the tomato sauce and the chiles; bring to a boil.
- Reduce the heat and simmer, uncovered, until the flavors are blended and the mixture thickens, slightly, about 5 minutes.
- Remove from the heat and stir in the cheddar cheese.
- Meanwhile, wrap the tortillas in foil and place in the oven to warm for 10 minutes.
- Spoon about 1/2 cup of the filling into the center of each tortilla.
- Fold in the sides, then roll to enclose the filling.

- Place the chimichangas, seam-side down, on the baking sheet.
- Lightly spray the tops of the tortillas with nonstick spray.
- Bake until golden and crisp, about 20 minutes. Do not turn.

Nutritional Information

Serving Size: 1 (146 g)

Servings Per Recipe: 4

Amount Per Serving

Calories 95 Calories from Fat 6

% Daily Value

Total Fat 1g 1%

Saturated Fat 0g

Cholesterol 35mg 11%

Sodium 376mg 15%

Total Carbohydrate 7g 2%

Dietary Fiber 2g 7%

Sugars 4g 15%

Protein 15g 30%

LUNCH: 15

Sunshine Fruit Salad

Ingredients

- 15 oz can mandarin orange
- 20 oz can pineapple, chunks

- 1 oz package fat-free, sugar-free instant vanilla pudding mix

Directions

- Prep 3 min
- Cook 0 min
- Ready 3 min
- Do not drain fruit.
- Use pudding mix dry, do not add milk.
- Combine orange, pineapple and pudding mix and blend well. Chill about 1 hour.

Nutritional Information

Serving Size: 1 (165 g)

Servings Per Recipe: 6

Amount Per Serving

Calories 94 Calories from Fat 2

% Daily Value

Total Fat 0g

Saturated Fat 0g

Cholesterol 0mg

Sodium 2mg

Total Carbohydrate 24g 8%

Dietary Fiber 2g 8%

Sugars 21g 84%

Protein 1g 1%

LUNCH: 16

Tex Mex Stuffed Sweet Potato

Ingredients

- 4 small sweet potatoes
- 1 tsp. olive oil
- 1/2 sweet onion, sliced thin
- 1 red pepper, chopped
- 1 green pepper, chopped
- 2 tomatoes, chopped
- 4 cups spinach
- 1 cup canned black beans, drained
- 1/2 tsp. chili powder
- 1/2 tsp. cumin
- 1/2 tsp. garlic powder
- Salt and pepper
- 8 tbsp. reduced fat cheddar cheese

Directions

- Prep Time: 5 min
- Cook Time: 10 min
- Total Time: 15 MINUTES
- Preheat the oven to 400 degrees.
- Bake or microwave your potatoes. To bake, preheat the oven to 400 degrees. Clean the potatoes and pierce with a knife or fork. Place on a baking sheet and cook for 60 minutes or until soft and skin begins to wrinkle. To microwave, clean the potatoes and pierce with a knife or fork. Place on a microwave safe dish and cover with a damp paper towel. Cook for 5 minutes and then flip. Cook for another 5 minutes and check for doneness. Continue cooking in 5 minute intervals until soft.

- Meanwhile, heat the olive oil over medium heat. Add the onion and peppers. Sauté for 5-7 minutes or until softened. If burning, add 1-2 tbsp. of water.
- the tomatoes, spinach, black beans, chili powder, cumin, and garlic powder. Stir together and cook until spinach wilts.
- Cut open potatoes and stuff with vegetable filling. Top with 2 tbsp. cheese.

Nutritional Facts

Serving Size: 1 potato

Amount Per Serving

Calories 246

Calories from Fat 27

% Daily Value

Total Fat 3g 5%

Saturated Fat 1g 5%

Monounsaturated Fat 0g 0%

Polyunsaturated Fat 0g 0%

Cholesterol 4mg 1%

Sodium 442mg 19%

Total Carbohydrate 47g 15%

Dietary Fiber 11g 45%

Sugars 12g

Protein 12g

LUNCH: 17

Black Bean, Corn, and Salsa Dip

Ingredients

- 1 can (15 1/2 oz) black beans, rinsed & drained
- 1 cup frozen corn, kernels
- 1 can (14 1/2 oz) diced tomatoes, with basil, oregano and garlic
- 1/2 cup salsa

Directions

- Prep 5 min
- Cook 0 min
- Ready 5 min
- Rinse and drain beans.
- Add frozen corn (it will thaw in the bowl).
- Add can of tomatoes and the salsa.
- Mix well.

Nutritional Information

Serving Size: 1 (129 g)

Servings Per Recipe: 3

Amount Per Serving

Calories 255 Calories from Fat 13

% Daily Value

Total Fat 1g 2%

Saturated Fat 0g 1%

Cholesterol 0mg

Sodium 265mg 11%

Total Carbohydrate 52g 17%

Dietary Fiber 12g 48%

Sugars 1g 5%

Protein 14g 26%

LUNCH: 18

Stove Top Macaroni and Cheese

Ingredients

- 16 oz macaroni
- 2 cup skim milk, or 1% milk
- 1/4 cup flour
- 3/4 tsp salt
- 3/4 tsp onion powder
- 1 cup low-fat cheddar cheese
- 1/8 tsp hot sauce, or Tabasco
- 1 pepper

Directions

- Prep 5 min
- Cook 10 min
- Ready 15 min
- Cook macaroni according to package directions. Drain.
- While macaroni is cooking, in a large saucepan over medium heat, whisk together milk, flour, salt, onion powder and pepper until blended.
- Bring to a boil, stirring occasionally.
- Reduce heat to a simmer, stirring often until thickened (2 to 5 minutes).
- Remove from heat; stir in cheese and hot sauce.
- Toss cooked macaroni with sauce.

Nutritional Information

Serving Size: 1 (183 g)

Servings Per Recipe: 6

Amount Per Serving

Calories 368 Calories from Fat 24

% Daily Value

Total Fat 3g 4%

Saturated Fat 1g 5%

Cholesterol 6mg 1%

Sodium 462mg 19%

Total Carbohydrate 66g 21%

Dietary Fiber 3g 10%

Sugars 2g 8%

Protein 18g 36%

LUNCH: 19

Mexican Pork Chops with Veggies

Ingredients

- 16 oz boneless pork cutlets or pork chops
- 1 green bell pepper, chopped
- 1 onion, chopped
- 1 can (14.5 oz) stewed tomatoes, or diced tomatoes & green chilies
- 2 cup corn
- 1/2 cup salsa

- 1 1/2 tsp oregano
- 1/2 tsp ground cumin

Directions

- Prep 10 min
- Cook 50 min
- Ready 60 min
- Preheat oven to 350.
- Brown pork chops in a hot skillet sprayed with cooking spray, approximately two minutes per side. Transfer the pork to a large casserole dish.
- Spray the same skillet with cooking spray, add the peppers and onions, and cook until tender. Add all the remaining ingredients and cook, stirring often, for about five minutes or until heated through.
- Pour the corn/tomato mixture from the skillet over the pork chops.
- Cover with foil, and bake for 45-50 minutes or until pork is cooked through.

Nutritional Information

Serving Size: 1 (381 g)

Servings Per Recipe: 4

Amount Per Serving

Calories 265 Calories from Fat 35

% Daily Value

Total Fat 4g 6%

Saturated Fat 1g 5%

Cholesterol 63mg 20%

Sodium 833mg 34%

Total Carbohydrate 31g 10%

Dietary Fiber 4g 15%

Sugars 6g 21%

Protein 30g 60%

LUNCH: 20

Chicken Enchiladas

Ingredients

- 2 cup cooked chicken, chopped
- 4 oz can diced green chiles
- 8 oz can green chili salsa
- 1/2 tsp salt
- 2 cup fat-free half-and-half
- 1/4 cup oil, for frying tortillas
- 12 corn tortilla
- 2 cup reduced-fat monterey jack cheese, shredded

Directions

Prep 20 min

Cook 20 min

Ready 40 min

- Preheat oven to 350°F.
- Mix chicken, chilies and salsa in a small bowl.
- Mix the salt and cream in a large shallow dish.
- Heat the Oil in a frying pan over med-high heat.
- Fry the tortillas one at a time for a few seconds til they start to blister and turn soft.
- Immediately dip each one in the cream mixture.

- Put a large dollop of the chicken mixture on each tortilla and roll it up.
- Place in an ungreased baking pan; flap side down.
- Pour remaining cream over roll enchiladas; sprinkle cheese over top.
- Bake uncovered 20 minutes for 20 minutes, or till heated through.

Nutritional Information

Serving Size: 1 (279 g)

Servings Per Recipe: 6

Amount Per Serving

Calories 390   Calories from Fat 156

% Daily Value

Total Fat 17g 26%

Saturated Fat 5g 22%

Cholesterol 47mg 15%

Sodium 1048mg 43%

Total Carbohydrate 33g 10%

Dietary Fiber 4g 15%

Sugars 6g 25%

Protein 26g 52%

LUNCH: 21

Slow Cooker Cheeseburger Soup

Ingredients

- 1 clove (medium sized) garlic, minced
- 1 medium onion, chopped
- 1 stalk (medium sized) celery, chopped
- 1 lb uncooked lean (93%) ground beef
- 2 tbsp all-purpose flour
- 3 cup canned chicken broth, divided
- 1 cup low-fat evaporated milk
- 8 oz reduced fat velveeta cheese, cubed
- 1/2 tsp paprika
- 1/4 tsp table salt
- 1/8 tsp black pepper
- 24 baked corn tortilla chips, crumbled
- 1 cooking spray

Directions

- Prep 15 min
- Cook 120 min
- Ready 135 min
- Coat a large nonstick skillet with cooking spray and heat over medium-high heat for about 30 seconds.
- Add garlic, onion and celery to skillet; cook, stirring frequently, until vegetables are tender, about 5 to 10 minutes.
- Coat a 3 quart or larger slow cooker with cooking spray; spoon in vegetables.
- Place same skillet over medium-high heat and brown beef, breaking up meat with a wooden spoon as it cooks, about 5 to 6 minutes; pour off any liquid and add meat to the slow cooker.
- In a small cup, combine flour and 1/2 cup of broth; stir until lump free.
- Pour flour mixture into skillet; add remaining 2 1/2 cups of broth.
- Bring to a simmer, scraping up any browned bits in bottom of skillet with a wooden spoon, then pour into the slow

cooker. Stir in evaporated milk, cheese, paprika, salt and pepper.
- Cover slow cooker and cook on Low setting for 2 hours.
- Serve soup topped with crumbled tortilla chips.
- Note: If the soup cooks too long, the cheese could separate.
- If that happens, combine 1 tablespoon of all-purpose flour and 1/4 cup of soup in a cup; stir to a paste.

Nutritional Information

Serving Size: 1 (201 g)

Servings Per Recipe: 8

Amount Per Serving

Calories 208 Calories from Fat 87

% Daily Value

Total Fat 10g 15%

Saturated Fat 5g 23%

Cholesterol 50mg 16%

Sodium 1150mg 47%

Total Carbohydrate 7g 2%

Dietary Fiber 1g 1%

Sugars 3g 13%

Protein 22g 42%

LUNCH: 22

Ham Steak with Pineapple Sauce

Ingredients

- 1 lb reduced sodium ham, 1 slice, about 1/2 inch thick
- 1 tbsp lemon juice
- 2 tsp brown sugar
- 1 tsp dijon mustard
- 1/8 tsp ground ginger
- 1/2 cup pineapple juice
- 1 tsp corn starch

Directions

- Prep 5 min
- Cook 6 min
- Ready 11 min
- Trim fat from the ham.
- Lightly score the ham slice in a diamond pattern using a sharp knife.
- Place in an 11 x 7 inch baking dish.
- Whisk together lemon juice, brown sugar, mustard, and ground ginger in a bowl and spread mixture over the ham.
- Cover with heavy-duty plastic wrap and vent.
- Microwave on High for 4 minutes or until thoroughly heated.
- Remove ham from the dish and cut into 4 equal pieces. Set aside and keep warm.
- Mix pineapple juice and corn starch in a glass measuring cup and stir well.
- Microwave on High for 1 1/2 minutes or until thick and bubbly. Stir well.
- Serve pineapple sauce with ham.

Nutritional Information

Serving Size: 1 (152 g)

Servings Per Recipe: 4

Amount Per Serving

Calories 225 Calories from Fat 85

% Daily Value

Total Fat 10g 14%

Saturated Fat 3g 15%

Cholesterol 66mg 21%

Sodium 1115mg 46%

Total Carbohydrate 8g 2%

Dietary Fiber 0g

Sugars 6g 21%

Protein 26g 50%

LUNCH: 23

Greek Penne Pasta

Ingredients

- 12 oz uncooked penne pasta
- 1 tsp olive oil
- 2/3 oz pine nuts, about 2 tbsp
- 1 1/2 tsp garlic, minced
- 10 oz chopped frozen spinach, thawed
- 1 lb plum tomato, chopped
- 4 oz feta cheese, crumbled
- 6 piece medium olives, pitted and chopped

Directions

- Prep 15 min
- Cook 20 min
- Ready 35 min

- Cook pasta according to package directions (without butter or oil), drain and set aside.
- Coat a large skillet with cooking spray.
- Add olive oil and heat over medium-high heat until oil sizzles.
- Add pine nuts and garlic.
- Cook and stir until pine nuts are golden brown, about 3 minutes.
- Stir in spinach and tomatoes and cook until heated through, stirring occasionally, about 3 minutes.
- Add spinach mixture to pasta and toss until combined.
- Serve pasta sprinkled with feta cheese and olives.

Nutritional Information

Serving Size: 1 (156 g)

Servings Per Recipe: 8

Amount Per Serving

Calories 238 Calories from Fat 62

% Daily Value

Total Fat 7g 10%

Saturated Fat 3g 13%

Cholesterol 13mg 4%

Sodium 223mg 9%

Total Carbohydrate 39g 12%

Dietary Fiber 7g 26%

Sugars 2g 9%

Protein 8g 14%

LUNCH: 24

Cheesy Chicken Enchiladas

Ingredients

- 8 oz reduced-fat velveeta cheese
- 1/2 cup fat-free sour cream
- 1/4 cup fat-free evaporated milk
- 1/4 cup scallion, green part only, minced
- 1/4 tsp crushed red pepper flakes
- 3 cup cooked chicken breast, chopped
- 6 medium sized whole wheat tortilla, 7 inches each
- 1/4 cup sharp low-fat cheddar cheese, shredded
- 6 medium black olives, pitted, sliced
- 1/4 cup salsa
- 1 cooking spray, 1 spray

Directions

- Prep 15 min
- Cook 27 min
- Ready 42 min
- Preheat oven to 350 degrees F (175 degrees C).
- Coat a 9 inch glass baking dish with cooking spray.
- In a microwave-safe bowl, combine velveeta and sour cream; cover and microwave on high power until cheese melts, about 1 1/2 to 2 minutes. Remove half of the melted cheese to a small bowl and stir in evaporated milk; set aside.
- Add scallions, red pepper flakes and chicken to remaining cheese mixture; stir to coat.
- Spoon about 2/3 cup of the chicken mixture down the center of each tortilla; fold in the sides of the tortilla to cover the filling and place tortillas in a single layer in the prepared dish.

- Spoon remaining cheese sauce over the top of the enchiladas, then sprinkle with shredded cheddar cheese and olives.
- Bake until cheese topping is bubbly, about 20 to 25 minutes. Serve with salsa

Nutritional Information

Serving Size: 1 (163 g)

Servings Per Recipe: 6

Amount Per Serving

Calories 266 Calories from Fat 94

% Daily Value

Total Fat 11g 16%

Saturated Fat 5g 23%

Cholesterol 78mg 25%

Sodium 796mg 33%

Total Carbohydrate 10g 3%

Dietary Fiber 0g 1%

Sugars 6g 25%

Protein 31g 62%

LUNCH: 25

Mini Chocolate Chip Cookies

Ingredients

- 2 tbsp butter, softened
- 2 tsp canola oil
- 1/2 cup dark brown sugar
- 1 tsp vanilla extract
- 1/8 tsp salt
- 1 large egg white
- 3/4 cup all-purpose flour
- 1/4 tsp baking soda
- 3 oz semi-sweet chocolate chips

Directions

- Prep 10 min
- Cook 6 min
- Ready 16 min
- Preheat oven to 375 degrees F (190 degrees C).
- In a medium bowl, cream butter, oil, and brown sugar together.
- Add vanilla extract, salt, and egg white. Mix thoroughly.

- Mix flour and baking soda and add to creamed mixture. Mix well.
- Add chocolate chips and stir to distribute evenly.
- Drop dough by rounded half teaspoons on a nonstick baking sheet.
- Bake cookies for 4-6 minutes.
- Cool on a wire rack.

Nutritional Information

Serving Size: 1 (15 g)

Servings Per Recipe: 24

Amount Per Serving

Calories 63 Calories from Fat 29

% Daily Value

Total Fat 3g 5%

Saturated Fat 2g 9%

Cholesterol 3mg

Sodium 38mg 1%

Total Carbohydrate 9g 2%

Dietary Fiber 1g 2%

Sugars 5g 18%

Protein 1g 2%

LUNCH: 26

Mexican Hot Chocolate

Ingredients

4 cup non-fat milk

1/3 cup dark brown sugar, packed

1/4 cup unsweetened cocoa powder

1 oz semi-sweet or bittersweet chocolate, chopped

1/4 tsp ground cinnamon

Directions

- Prep 2 min
- Cook 6 min
- Ready 8 min
- Whisk together the milk, brown sugar, cocoa, chocolate, and cinnamon in a medium saucepan until well blended.
- Cook over medium heat, stirring often, until the mixture is hot and chocolate is melted, 5-6 minutes.

Nutritional Information

Serving Size: 1 (276 g)

Servings Per Recipe: 4

Amount Per Serving

Calories 202 Calories from Fat 42

% Daily Value

Total Fat 5g 7%

Saturated Fat 3g 14%

Cholesterol 5mg 1%

Sodium 111mg 4%

Total Carbohydrate 36g 11%

Dietary Fiber 3g 12%

Sugars 30g 121%

Protein 10g 20%

LUNCH: 27

Slow Cooker Crustless Apple Pie

Ingredients

- 10 large apple, I used Granny Smith
- 1 cup Splenda sugar substitute, or regular sugar if you prefer
- 1/2 cup water
- 2 tbsp cinnamon, more or less to taste

Directions

- Prep 15 min
- Cook 300 min
- Ready 315 min
- Peel and cut apples into chunks and place in a crock pot.
- In a small bowl, mix Splenda, water and cinnamon.
- Pour mixture over apples.
- Cook on Low setting for 4-5 hours, stirring occasionally.
- Serve warm with ice cream or whipped topping, if desired.

Nutritional Information

Serving Size: 1 (302 g)

Servings Per Recipe: 8

Amount Per Serving

Calories 174 Calories from Fat 4

% Daily Value

Total Fat 1g

Saturated Fat 0g

Cholesterol 0mg

Sodium 3mg

Total Carbohydrate 47g 15%

Dietary Fiber 8g 30%

Sugars 35g 139%

Protein 1g 1%

LUNCH: 28

Chinese General's Chicken

Ingredients

- 3/4 cup chicken broth
- 2 tbsp corn starch
- 2 tbsp granular Splenda sugar substitute
- 2 tbsp soy sauce
- 1 tbsp white wine vinegar
- 1/2 tsp ground ginger
- 2 tsp olive oil
- 2 medium scallion, chopped
- 2 tsp garlic, minced
- 1/2 tsp red pepper flakes
- 1 lb boneless, skinless chicken breast
- 2 cup brown rice, cooked

Directions

- Prep 10 min
- Cook 10 min
- Ready 20 min

- Cut chicken into 2 inch pieces.
- In a small bowl, mix together chicken broth, cornstarch, Splenda, soy sauce, vinegar and ginger. Set aside.
- Heat oil in a skillet or wok over medium-high heat. Add scallions, garlic and pepper. Cook 2 for minutes, then add chicken and cook until browned, about 5 more minutes.
- Add sauce and simmer until it thickens and chicken is cooked through, about 3 minutes.
- Serve chicken and sauce over rice.

Nutritional Information

Serving Size: 1 (281 g)

Servings Per Recipe: 4

Amount Per Serving

Calories 292 Calories from Fat 57

% Daily Value

Total Fat 6g 9%

Saturated Fat 1g 6%

Cholesterol 73mg 24%

Sodium 777mg 32%

Total Carbohydrate 29g 9%

Dietary Fiber 2g 8%

Sugars 1g 2%

Protein 29g 57%

LUNCH: 29

Vegetable Soup

Ingredients

- 6 cup non-fat beef broth
- 3 cup green cabbage, diced
- 1 1/3 cup carrot, sliced
- 1 cup onion, diced
- 4 garlic cloves, minced
- 1 cup green beans
- 2 tbsp tomato paste
- 3 stalk celery, diced
- 1 bell pepper, diced
- 2 cup mushrooms, sliced
- 2 cup broccoli, chopped

Directions

- Prep 20 min
- Cook 60 min
- Ready 80 min
- Add all the ingredients into a large pot or slow-cooker.
- Feel free to add any other Zero Points Vegetables (Weight Watchers).
- Simmer until veggies are cooked.
- Season to taste.
- Note: Depending on my mood I will exchange the Beef broth for Fat-Free Chicken Broth or Fat-Free Vegetable Broth.

Nutritional Information

Serving Size: 1 (143 g)

Servings Per Recipe: 12

Amount Per Serving

Calories 33 Calories from Fat 2

% Daily Value

Total Fat 0g

Saturated Fat 0g

Cholesterol 0mg

Sodium 49mg 2%

Total Carbohydrate 7g 2%

Dietary Fiber 2g 9%

Sugars 3g 13%

Protein 2g 3%

LUNCH: 30

Mexican Watermelon Agua Fresca

Ingredients

- 8 cup seedless watermelon, cut into chunks
- 1 cup cold water

- 2 tbsp sugar
- 2 tbsp fresh lime juice
- 6 small wedges watermelon, for garnish

Directions

- Prep 10 min
- Cook 0 min
- Ready 10 min
- Combine 4 cups of the watermelon cubes and 1/2 cup of the water in a blender and puree. Press the mixture through a sieve set over a medium bowl. Pour into a large pitcher. Repeat with the remaining watermelon and water.
- Add the sugar and lime juice to the pitcher; stir until the sugar is dissolved.
- Pour the agua fresca into 6 ice-filled glasses. Garnish each drink with a watermelon wedge.

Nutritional Information

Serving Size: 1 (253 g)

Servings Per Recipe: 6

Amount Per Serving

Calories 79 Calories from Fat 2

% Daily Value

Total Fat 0g

Saturated Fat 0g

Cholesterol 0mg

Sodium 3mg

Total Carbohydrate 20g 6%

Dietary Fiber 1g 3%

Sugars 17g 68%

Protein 1g 2%

CHAPTER SIX
30 RECIPES FOR DINNER
DINNER: 01

15 Minute Lemon and Herb Shrimp

Ingredients

- 2 tsp olive oil
- 1 lb large shrimp , peeled and deveined
- 2 tbsp fresh lemon juice
- 1 tsp Spice Islands salt-free lemon & herb seasoning , or other brand
- 1/2 tsp table salt
- 1/4 tsp black pepper, freshly ground
- 2 tbsp fresh parsley, chopped

Directions

- Prep 10 min
- Cook 5 min
- Ready 15 min
- Heat oil in a large skillet over medium heat. Add shrimp and sauté 1 minute. Add lemon juice, lemon herb seasoning, salt and pepper; stir to coat shrimp. Sauté until shrimp are bright pink and cooked through, about 3 minutes more.
- Remove from heat and stir in parsley.

Nutritional Information

Serving Size: 1 (126 g)

Servings Per Recipe: 4

Amount Per Serving

Calories 103 Calories from Fat 30

% Daily Value

Total Fat 3g 5%

Saturated Fat 0g 2%

Cholesterol 143mg 47%

Sodium 934mg 38%

Total Carbohydrate 2g

Dietary Fiber 0g

Sugars 0g

Protein 16g 31%

DINNER: 02

Spicy Baked Shrimp

Ingredients

- 2 tbsp lemon juice
- 1 tbsp honey
- 2 tsp dried parsley
- 2 tsp creole seasoning
- 1 tsp olive oil
- 2 tsp low-sodium soy sauce
- 1 lb large shrimp , peeled and deveined
- 1 olive oil-flavored cooking spray

Directions

- Prep 5 min
- Cook 8 min
- Ready 13 min
- Preheat oven to 450 degrees F (230 degrees C).
- Coat an 11 x 7 inch baking dish with cooking spray.

- Add lemon juice, honey, dried parsley, creole seasoning, olive oil, and soy sauce to dish and stir well to combine.
- Add shrimp and toss to coat.
- Bake for 8 minutes or until shrimp turn pink, stirring occasionally.

Nutritional Information

Amount Per Serving

Calories 111 Calories from Fat 20

% Daily Value

Total Fat 2g 3%

Saturated Fat 0g 1%

Cholesterol 143mg 47%

Sodium 813mg 33%

Total Carbohydrate 6g 2%

Dietary Fiber 0g

Sugars 5g 18%

Protein 16g 31%

DINNER: 03

Dijon Fish Fillets

Ingredients

- 1 (8 ounce) orange roughy, flounder, perch or sole fillet
- 1 tbsp dijon mustard
- 1 1/2 tsp lemon juice
- 1 tsp reduced-sodium Worcestershire sauce
- 2 tbsp Italian seasoned bread crumbs

- 1 butter-flavored cooking spray

Directions

- Prep 3 min
- Cook 12 min
- Ready 15 min
- Preheat oven to 450 degrees F (230 degrees C).
- Arrange fillet in an 11 x 7 inch baking dish coated with cooking spray.
- Combine mustard, lemon juice, and Worcestershire sauce, stirring well; spread mixture evenly over fillet.
- Sprinkle breadcrumbs evenly over fish.
- Bake uncovered for 12 minutes or until fish flakes easily when tested with a fork.
- Cut fillet in half and serve immediately.

Nutritional Information

Amount Per Serving

Calories 125 Calories from Fat 13

% Daily Value

Total Fat 2g 2%

Saturated Fat 0g

Cholesterol 72mg 23%

Sodium 299mg 12%

Total Carbohydrate 6g 1%

Dietary Fiber 1g 2%

Sugars 1g 2%

Protein 21g 41%

DINNER: 04

Egg Drop Soup with Chicken

Ingredients

- 4 cup low sodium chicken broth, (use a good quality stock)
- 1/2 tsp soy sauce
- 1/2 cup cooked boneless, skinless chicken breast, chopped
- 1/2 cup frozen green peas, (baby peas are nice)
- 1/4 cup green onion, thinly sliced
- 1 egg, lightly beaten

Directions

- Prep 5 min
- Cook 5 min
- Ready 10 min
- In saucepan, bring chicken stock and soy sauce to a boil. Add chicken, peas and green onion; bring to a boil again.
- Remove from heat; drizzle in egg in slow steady stream. Let sit for 1 minute for egg to set.
- Stir gently before ladling into bowls.

Nutritional Information

Amount Per Serving

Calories 119 Calories from Fat 37

% Daily Value

Total Fat 4g 6%

Saturated Fat 1g 6%

Cholesterol 61mg 20%

Sodium 181mg 7%

Total Carbohydrate 8g 2%

Dietary Fiber 2g 6%

Sugars 2g 8%

Protein 14g 27%

DINNER: 05

Parmesan Chicken Cutlets

Ingredients

- 1/4 cup parmesan cheese, grated
- 2 tbsp dried seasoned Italian bread crumbs
- 1/8 tsp paprika
- 1 tsp dried parsley
- 1/2 tsp garlic powder
- 1/4 tsp black pepper, freshly ground
- 4 boneless chicken breast, about 1 pound

Directions

- Prep 10 min
- Cook 25 min
- Ready 35 min
- Preheat oven to 400 degrees.
- In resealable plastic bag, combine cheese, crumbs and all seasonings; shake well.
- Transfer mixture to plate; dip each chicken breast in cheese mixture, turning to coat all sides.
- Arrange on nonstick baking sheet.
- Bake until chicken is cooked through, 20-25 minutes.

Nutritional Information

Amount Per Serving

Calories 173 Calories from Fat 44

% Daily Value

Total Fat 5g 7%

Saturated Fat 2g 8%

Cholesterol 78mg 26%

Sodium 294mg 12%

Total Carbohydrate 3g 1%

Dietary Fiber 0g 1%

Sugars 0g 1%

Protein 27g 54%

DINNER: 06

Baked Chicken with Lemon and Herbs

Ingredients

- 1 lb boneless, skinless chicken breast, four 4 oz halves
- 1/2 tsp sea salt
- 1/4 tsp black pepper, freshly ground
- 1 tsp olive oil
- 2 tsp fresh lemon juice, or to taste
- 2 tsp fresh rosemary, chopped
- 2 tsp fresh parsley, chopped
- 1/4 cup chicken broth
- 1 medium lemon, quartered, for garnish (optional)

Directions

- Prep 10 min
- Cook 35 min

- Ready 45 min
- Preheat oven to 400 degrees F (200 degrees C).
- Season both sides of chicken with sea salt and black pepper. Place in a small, shallow roasting pan and drizzle with olive oil. Sprinkle with lemon juice, rosemary, and parsley. Pour broth around the chicken to coat the bottom of the pan.
- Bake for 30 to 35 minutes or until the chicken is cooked through. Garnish with fresh lemon, if desired.

Nutritional Information

Serving Size: 1 (141 g)

Servings Per Recipe: 4

Amount Per Serving

Calories 146 Calories from Fat 37

% Daily Value

Total Fat 4g 6%

Saturated Fat 1g 4%

Cholesterol 73mg 24%

Sodium 470mg 19%

Total Carbohydrate 1g

Dietary Fiber 0g 1%

Sugars 0g 1%

Protein 25g 49%

DINNER: 07
Oven Fried Pork Chops

Ingredients

- 6 oz center-cut lean pork loin chop
- 2 tbsp pineapple juice
- 1 tbsp low-sodium soy sauce
- 1/4 tsp ground ginger
- 1/8 tsp garlic powder
- 1 large egg white, lightly beaten
- 1/3 cup dry bread crumbs
- 1/4 tsp dried Italian seasoning
- 1/4 tsp paprika
- 1 dash garlic powder
- 1 cooking spray

Directions

- Prep 15 min
- Cook 50 min
- Ready 65 min
- Preheat oven to 350 degrees.
- Trim fat from chops.
- Combine juice, soy sauce, ginger, garlic powder and egg whites in a bowl; stir well.
- Combine breadcrumbs, Italian seasoning, paprika, and dash of garlic powder in a shallow dish; stir well.
- Dip chops in juice mixture, and dredge in breadcrumbs mixture.
- Place chops on a broiler pan coated with cooking spray.
- Bake at 350 degrees for 50 minutes or until tender, turning after 25 minutes.

Nutritional Information

Serving Size: 1 (96 g)

Servings Per Recipe: 4

Amount Per Serving

Calories 133 Calories from Fat 27

% Daily Value

Total Fat 3g 4%

Saturated Fat 1g 4%

Cholesterol 46mg 15%

Sodium 252mg 10%

Total Carbohydrate 8g 2%

Dietary Fiber 1g 2%

Sugars 2g 5%

Protein 17g 34%

DINNER: 08

Roasted Pork Tenderloin with Herbs

Ingredients

- 1 cooking spray
- 2 tsp dried thyme
- 2 tsp dried oregano
- 1 tsp garlic powder
- 1 tsp onion powder
- 1 tsp table salt
- 1 tsp black pepper, freshly ground
- 2 tsp olive oil
- 2 lb lean pork tenderloin

Directions

- Prep 5 min
- Cook 30 min

- Ready 35 min
- Preheat oven to 400°F. Coat a shallow roasting pan with cooking spray.
- Combine thyme, oregano, garlic powder, onion powder, salt and pepper in a small bowl; set aside.
- Rub oil all over pork. Sprinkle thyme mixture all over pork and transfer to prepared pan.
- Roast until an instant-read thermometer inserted in center of pork reads 160°F, about 30 minutes.
- Let stand 10 minutes before slicing crosswise into thin (about 1/2-inch thick) slices.

Nutritional Information

Serving Size: 1 (116 g)

Servings Per Recipe: 8

Amount Per Serving

Calories 151 Calories from Fat 46

% Daily Value

Total Fat 5g 7%

Saturated Fat 2g 7%

Cholesterol 74mg 24%

Sodium 350mg 14%

Total Carbohydrate 1g

Dietary Fiber 0g 1%

Sugars 0g

Protein 24g 47%

DINNER: 09

Lemon Pepper Chicken Breasts

Ingredients

- 2 tbsp lemon pepper seasoning,
- 1 tbsp all-purpose flour
- 4 (3 oz each) boneless, skinless chicken breast
- 1 tbsp unsalted butter
- 1/2 medium lemon, zested and juiced
- 1 cup low-sodium chicken broth

Directions

- Prep 10 min
- Cook 25 min
- Ready 35 min
- On a large plate, combine lemon pepper seasoning with flour. Pat chicken dry and coat with flour mixture. Heat butter in a large skillet, add chicken, and brown for about 3 minutes per side.
- Mix together lemon zest and juice with broth. Pour over chicken, cover, and cook for 15 minutes. Remove lid and cook for another 5 minutes or until juices run clear.

Nutritional Information

Serving Size: 1 (150 g)

Servings Per Recipe: 4

Amount Per Serving

Calories 139 Calories from Fat 49

% Daily Value

Total Fat 6g 8%

Saturated Fat 2g 12%

Cholesterol 62mg 20%

Sodium 117mg 4%

Total Carbohydrate 2g

Dietary Fiber 0g

Sugars 0g

Protein 20g 38%

DINNER: 10

Slow Cooker Chili

4/29/22

Ingredients

- 1 lb extra-lean ground beef, or ground turkey
- 1 tbsp fresh garlic, minced
- 1 large red bell pepper, seeded and diced

- 1 large green bell pepper, seeded and diced
- 2 tbsp chili powder
- 2 tsp cumin
- 1 can (28 oz) crushed tomatoes
- 1 can (15 oz) red kidney beans, drained and rinsed
- 1 sweet onion, chopped
- 1/4 cup canned diced green chiles, or 1 fresh jalapeno pepper, seeded and finely chopped
- 2 tbsp tomato paste
- 1 black pepper, to taste

Directions

- Prep 20 min
- Cook 300 min
- Ready 320 min
- Cook ground beef or turkey and garlic in a nonstick skillet, breaking apart the meat, until well browned. Drain off any fat very well, then return to the pan. Add bell peppers and cook until softened, about 5 minutes. Stir in chili powder and cumin.
- Place tomatoes, kidney beans, onion, chilies or jalapeno, tomato paste, and meat mixture in a slow cooker and stir to combine. Cover and cook on High until flavors are blended, about 4-5 hours. Season to taste with black pepper.

Nutritional Information

Serving Size: 1 (184 g)

Servings Per Recipe: 12

Amount Per Serving

Calories 138 Calories from Fat 23

% Daily Value

Total Fat 3g 4%

Saturated Fat 1g 4%

Cholesterol 23mg 7%

Sodium 158mg 6%

Total Carbohydrate 17g 5%

Dietary Fiber 5g 20%

Sugars 2g 8%

Protein 13g 26%

DINNER: 11

Tuna Salad

Ingredients

- 12 oz canned chunk solid white tuna in water, drained
- 1/2 cup celery, finely diced
- 2 tbsp fresh parsley, chopped
- 2 tbsp reduced calorie mayonnaise
- 1/2 tsp dijon mustard
- 1/2 tsp salt
- 1/4 tsp black pepper, freshly ground

Directions

- Prep 10 min
- Cook 0 min
- Ready 10 min
- Combine tuna, celery and parsley in a medium bowl. Add mayonnaise, mustard, salt and pepper; stir to combine.
- For a flavor boost without increasing the points value, you can add diced olives, chopped pickles or relish, or onions.

Nutritional Information

Serving Size: 1 (108 g)

Servings Per Recipe: 4

Amount Per Serving

Calories 137 Calories from Fat 45

% Daily Value

Total Fat 5g 7%

Saturated Fat 1g 5%

Cholesterol 38mg 12%

Sodium 689mg 28%

Total Carbohydrate 1g

Dietary Fiber 0g 1%

Sugars 1g 2%

Protein 20g 40%

DINNER: 12

Turkey Sausage and Bell Peppers

Ingredients

- 1/4 lb Italian turkey sausage, cut into 1/4 in. slices
- 1 red bell pepper, sliced
- 1 green bell pepper, sliced
- 1 yellow bell pepper, sliced
- 1 onion, sliced
- 1/4 cup chicken broth
- 2 tbsp garlic, minced
- 1/4 tsp crushed red pepper flakes
- 1/4 tsp dried oregano, leaves

Directions

- Prep 15 min
- Cook 10 min
- Ready 25 min
* Spray large skillet with Pam cooking spray and heat skillet.
* Add sausage and stir frequently until no longer pink 5-6 minutes.
* Add bell peppers,onion,broth, garlic, pepper flakes and oregano. Saute all together for 5 minutes or until liquid evaporates.
* Reduce heat and simmer covered 5 minutes more.

Nutritional Information

Serving Size: 1 (181 g)

Servings Per Recipe: 4

Amount Per Serving

Calories 93 Calories from Fat 25

% Daily Value

Total Fat 3g 4%

Saturated Fat 0g

Cholesterol 15mg 5%

Sodium 315mg 13%

Total Carbohydrate 12g 3%

Dietary Fiber 2g 9%

Sugars 4g 16%

Protein 6g 12%

DINNER: 13

Shrimp with Cilanto and Lime

Ingredients

- 1 3/4 lb large shrimp , peeled and deveined
- 2 tbsp fresh lime juice
- 1/2 tsp ground cumin
- 1/4 tsp ground ginger
- 2 garlic cloves, minced
- 1 tbsp olive oil
- 1/4 cup fresh cilantro, chopped
- 1 tsp lime, zest
- 1/2 tsp salt
- 1/4 tsp pepper

Directions

- Prep 15 min
- Cook 5 min
- Ready 20 min
- Combine shrimp, lime juice, cumin, ginger, and garlic in a large bowl; toss well.
- Heat oil in a large nonstick skillet over medium-high heat.
- Add shrimp mixture and saute for 4 minutes or until shrimp is done.
- Remove from heat; stir in cilantro, lime zest, salt, and pepper.

Nutritional Information

Serving Size: 1 (213 g)

Servings Per Recipe: 4

Amount Per Serving

Calories 177 Calories from Fat 49

% Daily Value

Total Fat 6g 8%

Saturated Fat 1g 3%

Cholesterol 251mg 83%

Sodium 1418mg 59%

Total Carbohydrate 3g 1%

Dietary Fiber 0g

Sugars 0g

Protein 27g 54%

DINNER: 14

Tuna Pasta Salad

Ingredients

- 6 oz pasta
- 1 can (12 oz) tuna in water, drained
- 1/2 cup yellow bell pepper, cut into strips
- 1/2 cup cherry tomato, halved
- 1/4 cup celery, diced
- 3/4 cup low-salt salsa
- 1/2 cup low-fat mayonnaise
- 1/2 tsp ground red pepper
- 2 tbsp scallion, sliced

Directions

- Prep 10 min
- Cook 15 min
- Ready 25 min

- Cook pasta according to package directions, omitting salt and fat.
- Drain pasta, rinse under cold water, and drain again.
- In a large bowl, combine pasta, tuna, bell pepper, cherry tomatoes, and celery.
- In a small bow, combine salsa, mayonnaise, and red pepper. Add dressing to the pasta mixture; toss. Cover and chill. Sprinkle with scallions before serving.

Nutritional Information

Serving Size: 1 (148 g)

Servings Per Recipe: 6

Amount Per Serving

Calories 194 Calories from Fat 20

% Daily Value

Total Fat 2g 3%

Saturated Fat 1g 2%

Cholesterol 24mg 7%

Sodium 414mg 17%

Total Carbohydrate 25g 8%

Dietary Fiber 2g 7%

Sugars 2g 8%

Protein 18g 35%

DINNER: 15

Chicken Spinach Crescent Ring

Ingredients

- 1 can (8 oz) reduced fat crescent roll dough, 8 rolls
- 4 tbsp reduced fat whipped cream cheese, softened
- 1 cup fresh baby spinach
- 5 oz cooked grilled chicken, strips
- 1/3 cup reduced fat shredded Mexican blend cheese

Directions

- Prep 15 min
- Cook 15 min
- Ready 30 min
- Preheat oven to 375 degrees F (190 degrees C).
- Arrange crescent rolls on an ungreased baking sheet with points facing outward towards the edge to create a ring. Spread cream cheese on crescent rolls and season with spices of your choice. Place spinach on top of cream cheese, evenly distribute grilled chicken strips, and sprinkle with Mexican cheese. Pull the point of each crescent roll up and over to wrap around the filling, then tuck underneath.
- Bake for 14 minutes or until crescent rolls are golden brown.

Nutritional Information

Serving Size: 1 (59 g)

Servings Per Recipe: 8

Amount Per Serving

Calories 142 Calories from Fat 47

% Daily Value

Total Fat 5g 8%

Saturated Fat 2g 11%

Cholesterol 35mg 11%

Sodium 208mg 8%

Total Carbohydrate 16g 5%

Dietary Fiber 1g 4%

Sugars 1g 5%

Protein 8g 15%

DINNER: 16

Easy Chicken and Dumplings

Ingredients

- 2 can (8 oz each) reduced-sodium, fat-free chicken broth
- 2 can (8 oz each) reduced-sodium, low-fat cream of chicken soup, such as Healthy Request
- 3 cup chicken breast, cooked and chopped
- 1/2 tsp celery salt
- 1 salt, to taste
- 1 black pepper, to taste
- 5 fat-free tortillas, cut into 2 inch pieces

Directions

- Prep 25 min
- Cook 30 min
- Ready 55 min
- Add chicken broth, cream of chicken soup, and cooked chicken breasts to a large saucepan and bring to a boil. Season with celery salt, salt, and pepper. When the liquid is boiling, carefully drop tortillas in one at a time. Reduce heat and simmer for 20-30 minutes.

Nutritional Information

Serving Size: 1 (54 g)

Servings Per Recipe: 8

Amount Per Serving

Calories 105 Calories from Fat 37

% Daily Value

Total Fat 4g 6%

Saturated Fat 1g 5%

Cholesterol 44mg 14%

Sodium 44mg 1%

Total Carbohydrate 0g

Dietary Fiber 0g

Sugars 0g

Protein 16g 31%

DINNER: 17

Mexican Chicken Breasts

Ingredients

- 1 package (1 1/4 oz) taco seasoning mix
- 4 (4 oz each) boneless, skinless chicken breast
- 1 cup salsa
- 1/4 cup fat-free sour cream

Directions

- Prep 3 min
- Cook 30 min
- Ready 33 min
- Place chicken breasts and taco seasoning in a seal able plastic bag; shake to coat well.
- Spray casserole dish with cooking spray
- Place breasts in casserole.

- Bake 30 minutes at 375 degrees.
- Top with salsa about 5 minutes before breasts are done.
- Top with sour cream before serving.

Nutritional Information

Serving Size: 1 (203 g)

Servings Per Recipe: 4

Amount Per Serving

Calories 178 Calories from Fat 29

% Daily Value

Total Fat 3g 5%

Saturated Fat 1g 3%

Cholesterol 74mg 24%

Sodium 1246mg 51%

Total Carbohydrate 12g 3%

Dietary Fiber 3g 10%

Sugars 5g 19%

Protein 26g 51%

DINNER: 18

Easy Cheesy Eggplant Casserole

Ingredients

- 1 cup spaghetti sauce
- 3/4 cup low-fat mozzarella cheese, shredded
- 3/4 cup non-fat cottage cheese

- 2 tbsp parmesan cheese, grated
- 3/4 lb eggplant, sliced 1/2-inch thick

Directions

- Prep 5 min
- Cook 40 min
- Ready 45 min
- Grill eggplant on George Foreman Grill for about 5-10 minutes until soft. Spray 8x8 baking pan with nonstick spray. Put eggplant on bottom of pan. Spread spaghetti sauce over eggplant. Mix cottage cheese and mozzarella, and spread it over sauce. Sprinkle with Parmesan cheese. Bake at 350º for 30-35 minutes and serve hot.

Nutritional Information

Serving Size: 1 (146 g)

Servings Per Recipe: 4

Amount Per Serving

Calories 79 Calories from Fat 16

% Daily Value

Total Fat 2g 2%

Saturated Fat 1g 3%

Cholesterol 5mg 1%

Sodium 261mg 10%

Total Carbohydrate 11g 3%

Dietary Fiber 4g 14%

Sugars 5g 21%

Protein 5g 10%

DINNER: 19

Sesame Chicken

Ingredients

- 2 tbsp sesame seeds, raw
- 1 tbsp water
- 1 tbsp low-sodium soy sauce
- 1 tbsp maple syrup
- 1 tbsp dry sherry
- 1 tsp fresh ginger root, minced
- 1/2 tsp five-spice powder spices
- 2 tbsp all-purpose flour
- 1/2 tsp salt
- 1/4 tsp black pepper
- 1 lb uncooked boneless skinless boneless, skinless chicken breast, cut into 2-inch strips
- 2 tsp peanut oil

Directions

- Prep 20 min
- Cook 11 min
- Ready 31 min
- Place a large nonstick skillet over medium-high heat. Add sesame seeds and cook until lightly toasted, shaking pan frequently, about 2 to 3 minutes; transfer seeds to a shallow dish and set aside.
- Whisk water, soy sauce, maple syrup, sherry, ginger and five-spice powder together in a small bowl; set aside.
- Combine flour, salt and pepper together in a shallow dish; add chicken and turn to coat. Shake chicken pieces to remove excess flour.
- Heat oil in a large nonstick skillet over medium-high heat. Add chicken and sauté until browned on all sides, about 5 minutes. Add soy sauce mixture to chicken and cook until

sauce thickens and is almost evaporated, about 2 to 3 minutes more.
- Dip chicken pieces in toasted sesame seeds and serve, drizzled with any additional soy sauce mixture.

Nutritional Information

Serving Size: 1 (142 g)

Servings Per Recipe: 4

Amount Per Serving

Calories 216 Calories from Fat 53

% Daily Value

Total Fat 6g 9%

Saturated Fat 1g 5%

Cholesterol 66mg 21%

Sodium 517mg 21%

Total Carbohydrate 8g 2%

Dietary Fiber 1g 2%

Sugars 3g 12%

Protein 28g 55%

DINNER: 20

Garlic Lemon Scallops

Ingredients

- 1 tbsp olive oil
- 1 1/4 lb sea scallop, dried with paper towels
- 2 tbsp all-purpose flour
- 1/4 tsp salt
- 4 to 6 garlic cloves, minced
- 1 scallion, finely chopped
- 1 pinch ground sage
- 1 lemon, juiced
- 2 tbsp parsley, chopped

Directions

- Prep 10 min
- Cook 5 min
- Ready 15 min
- In a large nonstick skillet, heat the oil.
- In a medium bowl, toss scallops with flour and salt.
- Place scallops in the skillet; add garlic, scallions, and sage.
- Saute until scallops are just opaque, about 3-4 minutes.
- Stir in lemon juice and parsley; remove from heat and serve immediately.

Nutritional Information

Serving Size: 1 (170 g)

Servings Per Recipe: 4

Amount Per Serving

Calories 151 Calories from Fat 37

% Daily Value

Total Fat 4g 6%

Saturated Fat 1g 3%

Cholesterol 34mg 11%

Sodium 705mg 29%

Total Carbohydrate 10g 3%

Dietary Fiber 0g 1%

Sugars 0g 1%

Protein 18g 35%

DINNER: 21

Grilled Salmon with Teriyaki Sauce

Ingredients

- 1/4 cup dry sherry
- 1/4 cup low-sodium soy sauce
- 1 tbsp brown sugar
- 1 tbsp rice wine vinegar
- 1 tsp garlic powder
- 1/2 tsp black pepper
- 1/8 tsp ground ginger

- 16 oz skinless salmon fillet, 1 inch thick
- 1 cooking spray

Directions

- Prep 35 min
- Cook 20 min
- Ready 55 min
- Combine sherry, soy sauce, brown sugar, vinegar, garlic powder, pepper and ginger in a shallow dish; stir well. Add fish; cover, and marinate in refrigerator 30 minutes.
- Coat grill rack with cooking spray; place on grill over medium-hot coals (350-400 degrees). Remove fish from marinade; reserve marinade.
- Place fish on grill rack or in a grill basket coated with cooking spray; grill, uncovered, 5 to 7 minutes on each side or until fish flakes easily when tested with a fork.
- Transfer fish to a serving platter, and keep warm.
- Place reserved marinade in a small saucepan; bring to a boil. Boil 5 minutes or until marinade becomes thick and syrupy.
- Spoon over fish; serve immediately.

Nutritional Information

Serving Size: 1 (149 g)

Servings Per Recipe: 4

Amount Per Serving

Calories 182 Calories from Fat 45

% Daily Value

Total Fat 5g 7%

Saturated Fat 1g 4%

Cholesterol 53mg 17%

Sodium 619mg 25%

Total Carbohydrate 6g 1%

Dietary Fiber 0g 1%

Sugars 4g 15%

Protein 24g 48%

DINNER: 22

Southwestern Pork Chops

Ingredients

- 1 vegetable oil cooking spray
- 4 oz lean boneless pork loin chop, trimmed
- 1/3 cup salsa
- 2 tbsp fresh lime juice
- 1/4 cup fresh cilantro, chopped (or parsley)

Directions

- Prep 2 min
- Cook 13 min
- Ready 15 min
- Coat a large nonstick skillet with cooking spray; place over high heat until hot.
- Press chops with palm of hand to flatten slightly; add to skillet and cook 1 minute on each side or until browned.
- Reduce heat to medium-low.
- Combine salsa and lime juice; pour over chops.
- Simmer, uncovered, 8 minutes or until chops are done.
- If desired, sprinkle chops with cilantro.

Nutritional Information

Serving Size: 1 (168 g)

Servings Per Recipe: 4

Amount Per Serving

Calories 184 Calories from Fat 71

% Daily Value

Total Fat 8g 12%

Saturated Fat 3g 13%

Cholesterol 76mg 25%

Sodium 184mg 7%

Total Carbohydrate 2g

Dietary Fiber 0g 1%

Sugars 1g 3%

Protein 25g 49%

DINNER: 23

Salsa Chicken

Ingredients

- 4 (6 oz each) boneless, skinless chicken breast
- 3/4 cup salsa
- 1/2 cup green onion, sliced
- 1/4 cup parmesan cheese, grated

Directions

- Prep 5 min
- Cook 40 min
- Ready 45 min
- Preheat oven to 350*F.

- Place chicken in an 11 × 7-inch baking dish coated with cooking spray. Spoon salsa evenly over chicken; top with green onions. Sprinkle with cheese.
- Cover and bake for 30 minutes.
- Uncover and bake an additional 10 minutes or until chicken is done.
- Serve with hot cooked rice or baked potatoes.

Nutritional Information

Serving Size: 1 (237 g)

Servings Per Recipe: 4

Amount Per Serving

Calories 238 Calories from Fat 56

% Daily Value

Total Fat 6g 9%

Saturated Fat 2g 10%

Cholesterol 114mg 38%

Sodium 586mg 24%

Total Carbohydrate 4g 1%

Dietary Fiber 1g 4%

Sugars 2g 7%

Protein 40g 78%

DINNER: 24

Honey Glazed Salmon with Wasabi

Ingredients

- 3 tbsp mirin
- 1 tbsp seasoned rice vinegar
- 1 tbsp low-sodium soy sauce
- 1 tbsp honey
- 1 tsp fresh ginger, peeled and minced
- 2 tsp wasabi, paste
- 1 lb salmon fillet, cut into 4 equal pieces
- 1/2 tsp salt
- 1/2 tsp pepper
- 1/4 cup scallion, thinly sliced

Directions

- Prep 5 min
- Cook 15 min
- Ready 20 min
- To make the sauce, bring mirin, vinegar, soy sauce, honey, ginger, and wasabi to boil in a small saucepan.
- Cook, stirring occasionally, over medium-high heat until the flavors are blended and the sauce is thickened, about 5 minutes.
- Remove from the heat, cover, and keep warm.
- Meanwhile, sprinkle salmon with salt and pepper.
- Spray a large nonstick skillet with nonstick spray and set over high heat.
- Add salmon and cook, turning once, until the fish is browned on the outside and opaque in the center, about 4 minutes on each side.
- Spoon sauce over the salmon. Sprinkle with scallions and serve.

Nutritional Information

Serving Size: 1 (141 g)

Servings Per Recipe: 4

Amount Per Serving

Calories 180 Calories from Fat 45

% Daily Value

Total Fat 5g 7%

Saturated Fat 1g 4%

Cholesterol 52mg 17%

Sodium 511mg 21%

Total Carbohydrate 6g 1%

Dietary Fiber 0g 1%

Sugars 5g 18%

Protein 24g 47%

DINNER: 25

Shrimp Scampi

Ingredients

- 4 tsp olive oil
- 1 1/4 lb medium shrimp , peeled (tails left on)
- 6 to 8 garlic cloves, minced
- 1/2 cup low-sodium chicken broth
- 1/2 cup dry white wine
- 1/4 cup fresh lemon juice
- 1/4 cup plus 1 tablespoon fresh parsley, minced
- 1/4 tsp salt
- 1/4 tsp black pepper, freshly ground
- 4 slice lemon

Directions

- Prep 25 min
- Cook 0 min
- Ready 25 min
- In a large nonstick skillet, heat the oil. Sauté the shrimp until just pink, 2-3 minutes.
- Add the garlic and cook stirring constantly, about 30 seconds.
- With a slotted spoon transfer the shrimp to a platter, keep hot.
- In the skillet, combine the broth, wine, lemon juice, 1/4 cup of the parsley, the salt and pepper; bring to a boil.
- Boil, uncovered, until the sauce is reduced by half; spoon over the shrimp.
- Serve garnished with the lemon slices and sprinkled with the remaining tablespoon of parsley.
- Note: I have also added scallops to this with great results!

Nutritional Information

Serving Size: 1 (238 g)

Servings Per Recipe: 4

Amount Per Serving

Calories 184 Calories from Fat 56

% Daily Value

Total Fat 6g 9%

Saturated Fat 1g 4%

Cholesterol 179mg 59%

Sodium 964mg 40%

Total Carbohydrate 6g 2%

Dietary Fiber 1g 2%

Sugars 1g 3%

Protein 21g 41%

DINNER: 26

Sweet and Sour Turkey Meatballs

Ingredients

- 1 lb ground turkey breast
- 1/2 green bell pepper, minced
- 4 scallion, thinly sliced
- 1/3 cup bread crumbs
- 1 egg white
- 1 tbsp reduced-sodium soy sauce
- 1/4 cup sweet and sour sauce
- 1/2 cup unsweetened applesauce

Directions

- Prep 10 min
- Cook 20 min
- Ready 30 min
- Preheat oven to 375 and spray a jelly roll pan with cooking spray.
- In a medium bowl, lightly combine turkey, pepper, scallions, bread crumbs, egg white and soy sauce. Shape into 32 balls (about 1") and place on the pan. Bake until cooked through and browned, about 15 minutes. (In my oven, at least, 20 minutes is best).
- In a microwave-safe bowl, combine sweet and sour sauce with applesauce. Microwave on high until hot and bubbly (about 2 minutes).
- Stir the meatballs into the sauce and serve.

Nutritional Information

Serving Size: 1 (209 g)

Servings Per Recipe: 4

Amount Per Serving

Calories 200 Calories from Fat 12

% Daily Value

Total Fat 1g 2%

Saturated Fat 0g 1%

Cholesterol 71mg 23%

Sodium 321mg 13%

Total Carbohydrate 15g 4%

Dietary Fiber 2g 5%

Sugars 6g 23%

Protein 31g 61%

DINNER: 27

Quick & Easy Salisbury Steak

Ingredients

- 1 lb extra lean ground beef
- 1/4 tsp garlic powder
- 1/2 tsp kosher salt
- 1/4 tsp black pepper
- 8 oz mushrooms, sliced
- 1/4 cup onion, minced
- 1 tsp dried thyme
- 2 tbsp dry sherry or white wine
- 1 jar (12 oz) jar fat-free beef gravy

Directions

- Prep 10 min
- Cook 10 min
- Ready 20 min
- Combine ground beef, garlic powder, salt and pepper, and mix well. Shape into 4 half-inch thick patties.
- Coat a large non-stick skillet with cooking spray, place over medium heat until hot. Add patties, cook 4 min per side or until they reach desired doneness. Remove from the skillet and set aside.
- Increase heat to medium-high, add mushrooms, onion and thyme to skillet, saute 3 minutes. Add sherry, saute 1 minute. Stir in gravy, return patties to skillet. Cook 2 minutes or until heated through.

Nutritional Information

Serving Size: 1 (274 g)

Servings Per Recipe: 4

Amount Per Serving

Calories 225 Calories from Fat 71

% Daily Value

Total Fat 8g 12%

Saturated Fat 4g 17%

Cholesterol 73mg 24%

Sodium 773mg 32%

Total Carbohydrate 8g 2%

Dietary Fiber 1g 5%

Sugars 2g 7%

Protein 29g 58%

DINNER: 28

Weight Watchers Chicken and Cheese Casserole

Ingredients

- 2 cup macaroni, cooked
- 2 cup boneless, skinless chicken breast, chopped
- 2 cup cream of mushroom soup, undiluted
- 2 cup skim milk
- 8 oz low-fat cheddar cheese, shredded

Directions

- Prep 10 min
- Cook 45 min
- Ready 55 min
- Preheat oven to 350 degrees F (175 degrees C).

- In a large casserole dish, combine macaroni, chicken breast, cream of mushroom soup, skim milk, and cheddar cheese, mixing well.
- Cover and bake for 35-45 minutes.
- Remove cover and bake for 10-15 minutes longer.

Nutritional Information

Serving Size: 1 (153 g)

Servings Per Recipe: 8

Amount Per Serving

Calories 153   Calories from Fat 38

% Daily Value

Total Fat 4g 6%

Saturated Fat 2g 9%

Cholesterol 7mg 2%

Sodium 423mg 17%

Total Carbohydrate 16g 5%

Dietary Fiber 1g 2%

Sugars 1g 3%

Protein 12g 23%

DINNER: 29

Cola Chicken

Ingredients

- 4 boneless, skinless chicken breast
- 1 cup ketchup

- 1 diet cola
- 1/2 cup onion, chopped, optional

Directions

- Prep 5 min
- Cook 60 min
- Ready 65 min
- In a skillet, mix ketchup and cola.
- Add chicken and onions.
- Bring to a boil and cover. Reduce heat to medium and let cook for 45 minutes.
- Remove lid and simmer until thickens.

Nutritional Information

Serving Size: 1 (198 g)

Servings Per Recipe: 4

Amount Per Serving

Calories 193 Calories from Fat 29

% Daily Value

Total Fat 3g 4%

Saturated Fat 1g 3%

Cholesterol 76mg 25%

Sodium 805mg 33%

Total Carbohydrate 15g 5%

Dietary Fiber 0g

Sugars 14g 54%

Protein 26g 52%

DINNER: 30

Chicken Fried Rice

Ingredients

- 1 cooking spray
- 4 large egg white
- 1/2 cup scallion, chopped, green and white parts
- 2 medium garlic cloves, minced
- 12 oz boneless skinless boneless, skinless chicken breast, cut into 1/2-inch cubes
- 1/2 cup carrot, diced
- 2 cup cooked brown rice, kept hot
- 1/2 cup frozen green peas, thawed
- 3 tbsp low-sodium soy sauce

Directions

- Prep 10 min
- Cook 15 min
- Ready 25 min

- Coat a large nonstick skillet with cooking spray and set pan over medium-high heat. Add egg whites and cook, until scrambled, stirring frequently, about 3 to 5 minutes; remove from pan and set aside.
- Offheat, recoat skillet with cooking spray and place back over medium-high heat. Add scallions and garlic; sauté 2 minutes. Add chicken and carrots; sauté until chicken is golden brown and cooked through, about 5 minutes.
- Stir in reserved cooked egg whites, cooked brown rice, peas and soy sauce; cook until heated through, stirring once or twice, about 1 minute.

Nutritional Information

Serving Size: 1 (194 g)

Servings Per Recipe: 6

Amount Per Serving

Calories 179 Calories from Fat 19

% Daily Value

Total Fat 2g 3%

Saturated Fat 0g 2%

Cholesterol 36mg 12%

Sodium 403mg 16%

Total Carbohydrate 21g 7%

Dietary Fiber 3g 11%

Sugars 2g 8%

Protein 18g 35%

CHAPTER SEVEN
10 SPECIAL RECIPES.
SPECIAL RECIPES: 01
Orange Chicken with Broccoli

Ingredients

- 4 tsp canola oil
- 1 lb boneless, skinless chicken breast, cut crosswise into 1/2 inch strips
- 1 tbsp fresh ginger, minced and peeled
- 2 cup broccoli, cut into florets
- 1/4 cup water
- 1/2 cup low sodium chicken broth
- 1/4 cup orange juice
- 3 tbsp reduced-sodium soy sauce
- 1 tsp corn starch
- 1 tbsp water
- 1 orange, peeled and sectioned

Directions

- Prep 15 min
- Cook 10 min
- Ready 25 min
- Heat oil in a nonstick skillet over medium-high heat. Add chicken and cook for 3 minutes. Add ginger and cook for 2 more minutes or until the chicken is cooked through. Transfer to a plate and set aside.
- In the same skillet, add broccoli and 1/4 cup water, stirring to scrape up the browned bits from the bottom of the pan. Cover and cook until the broccoli is tender-crisp, 3-4 minutes. Return chicken back to the skillet. Stir in chicken broth, orange juice, and soy sauce. Mix cornstarch with 1 tablespoon water, add to the pan and cook, stirring

frequently, until the sauce comes to a boil and thickens slightly. Add orange sections and cook until heated through.

Nutritional Information

Serving Size: 1 (260 g)

Servings Per Recipe: 4

Amount Per Serving

Calories 216 Calories from Fat 70

% Daily Value

Total Fat 8g 12%

Saturated Fat 1g 5%

Cholesterol 73mg 24%

Sodium 551mg 22%

Total Carbohydrate 10g 3%

Dietary Fiber 1g 3%

Sugars 5g 18%

Protein 27g 53%

SPECIAL RECIPES: 02
Orange Crumbed Baked Chicken

Ingredients

- 2 tbsp orange juice
- 2 tbsp dijon mustard
- 1/4 tsp salt
- 3/4 cup whole-wheat crackers, crumbled

- 1 tbsp orange zest, grated
- 1 shallot, finely chopped
- 1/4 tsp black pepper, freshly ground
- 12 oz boneless skinless chicken thigh

Directions

- Prep 20 min
- Cook 35 min
- Ready 55 min
- Preheat oven to 350 degrees. Spray a nonstick baking sheet with nonstick cooking spray.
- In a small bowl, combine the orange juice, mustard and salt. On a sheet of wax paper combine the cracker crumbs, orange zest, shallot, and pepper. Brush the chicken on both sides with the mustard mixture then dredge in the crumbs, firmly pressing the crumbs to coat both sides. Place the chicken on the baking sheet.
- Bake 15 minutes, turn over and bake until cooked through. 15 to 20 minutes longer.

Nutritional Information

Serving Size: 1 (113 g)

Servings Per Recipe: 4

Amount Per Serving

Calories 194 Calories from Fat 59

% Daily Value

Total Fat 7g 10%

Saturated Fat 2g 7%

Cholesterol 71mg 23%

Sodium 420mg 17%

Total Carbohydrate 15g 4%

Dietary Fiber 2g 9%

Sugars 1g 3%

Protein 19g 37%

SPECIAL RECIPES: 03
Recipes Matched with Savings

Ingredients

- 2 tbsp dark brown sugar, packed
- 1 tbsp paprika
- 1 tbsp chili powder
- 1 1/2 tsp ground cumin
- 1 tsp salt
- 1/4 tsp cayenne pepper
- 1/3 cup ketchup
- 1/4 cup cider vinegar
- 2 tbsp molasses
- 2 tsp Worcestershire sauce
- 1 1/2 lb pork tenderloin, trimmed of all visible fat
- 1 pepper, freshly ground, to taste

Directions

- Prep 10 min
- Cook 30 min
- Ready 40 min
- Spray the grill rack with nonstick spray; prepare the grill for indirect heating.
- Prepare the spice rub: combine brown sugar, paprika, chili powder, cumin, salt, cayenne, and pepper in bowl.
- Rub half of the mixture all over the pork and let stand for 15 minutes.

- Meanwhile, prepare the mop sauce: combine ketchup, vinegar, molasses, and Worcestershire sauce in a bowl.
- Rub the pork with the remaining spice rub.
- Place over the indirect heat section of the grill.
- Grill for 15 minutes.
- Turn the pork and grill until an instant-read thermometer inserted into the center of the meat registers 160 degrees F (71 degrees C), 12-15 minutes longer.
- Remove from the grill, cover loosely with foil, and let stand for 10 minutes before slicing.
- Serve with the mop sauce.

Nutritional Information

Serving Size: 1 (154 g)

Servings Per Recipe: 6

Amount Per Serving

Calories 199 Calories from Fat 40

% Daily Value

Total Fat 5g 6%

Saturated Fat 1g 7%

Cholesterol 74mg 24%

Sodium 641mg 26%

Total Carbohydrate 15g 4%

Dietary Fiber 1g 3%

Sugars 12g 46%

Protein 24g 48%

SPECIAL RECIPES: 04
Crock Pot Chicken Chili

Ingredients

- 12 oz boneless, skinless chicken breast, diced
- 1 envelope (1 3/8 oz) chili seasoning mix
- 1 qt canned tomatoes
- 1 can (15 oz) corn, undrained
- 1 can (15 oz) kidney beans, drained
- 1 green bell pepper, chopped
- 1 onion, chopped
- 1/2 cup salsa

Directions

- Prep 10 min
- Cook 480 min
- Ready 490 min
- Spray a nonstick skillet with cooking spray and sear the chicken.
- Add chicken, chili seasoning mix, tomatoes, corn, kidney beans, green bell pepper, onion, and salsa to a crock pot.
- Cover and cook on Low for 6 to 8 hours.

Nutritional Information

Serving Size: 1 (313 g)

Servings Per Recipe: 8

Amount Per Serving

Calories 160 Calories from Fat 17

% Daily Value

Total Fat 2g 2%

Saturated Fat 0g 2%

Cholesterol 27mg 9%

Sodium 483mg 20%

Total Carbohydrate 24g 7%

Dietary Fiber 6g 22%

Sugars 7g 27%

Protein 14g 28%

SPECIAL RECIPES: 05
Oven Fried Fish

Ingredients

- 1 1/2 lb fresh haddock, tilapia fillets, or other white fish
- 1/4 cup white or yellow cornmeal
- 1/4 cup dry plain or seasoned bread crumbs

- 1/2 tsp dried dill
- 1/2 tsp salt
- 1/8 tsp black pepper
- 1/2 tsp paprika
- 1/3 cup skim milk
- 3 tbsp butter, melted

Directions

- Prep 10 min
- Cook 10 min
- Ready 20 min
- Preheat oven to 450 degrees.
- In a shallow dish, like a pie plate, combine all dry ingredients.
- Place milk in another shallow dish.
- Dip fish in milk, then in crumb mixture.
- Place in pan coated with cooking spray.
- Drizzle with melted butter.
- Bake for 10 minute or until fish flakes apart with fork.

Nutritional Information

Serving Size: 1 (144 g)

Servings Per Recipe: 6

Amount Per Serving

Calories 196   Calories from Fat 61

% Daily Value

Total Fat 7g 10%

Saturated Fat 4g 19%

Cholesterol 90mg 30%

Sodium 583mg 24%

Total Carbohydrate 8g 2%

Dietary Fiber 1g 2%

Sugars 0g 1%

Protein 24g 48%

SPECIAL RECIPES: 06
Avocado and Tomato Pasta Salad

Ingredients

- 1 cup penne pasta
- 4 tbsp low-fat mayonnaise
- 1 1/2 tsp fresh lime juice, or lemon juice
- 1 1/2 cup baby plum tomato
- 1 ripe avocado
- 1/4 red onion
- 1 cooked chicken breast, chopped (optional)
- 1 handful fresh coriander, optional
- 1 pinch salt, optional

Directions

- Prep 5 min
- Cook 15 min
- Ready 20 min
- Cook the pasta according to package directions.
- Meanwhile, put mayonnaise and lime juice in a large bowl and stir to combine.
- Chop baby plum tomatoes and avocado and add to the bowl. Finely dice and add red onion. Add cooked chopped chicken, if using.
- When the pasta is cooked, drain it, then pour cold water over it for a few minutes to quickly cool it. Drain again and add it to the bowl.

- If using fresh coriander, finely chop as much as you like and sprinkle it over the top.
- Season with salt, if desired, and stir the pasta salad thoroughly to mix all the ingredients together.

Nutritional Information

Serving Size: 1 (177 g)

Servings Per Recipe: 2

Amount Per Serving

Calories 494 Calories from Fat 233

% Daily Value

Total Fat 26g 39%

Saturated Fat 4g 18%

Cholesterol 8mg 2%

Sodium 225mg 9%

Total Carbohydrate 64g 21%

Dietary Fiber 14g 57%

Sugars 7g 26%

Protein 8g 15%

SPECIAL RECIPES: 07
4 Ingredient Guacamole - Weight Watchers (1 Point)

Ingredients

- 2 avocado, peeled, pitted, and chopped

- 1 plum tomato, chopped
- 2 tbsp onion, finely chopped
- 1/4 tsp salt

Directions

- Prep 10 min
- Cook 0 min
- Ready 10 min
- Place avocado in a medium bowl and gently mash until chunky. Stir in tomato, onion, and salt. Serve immediately or press a piece of plastic wrap directly onto the surface of the guacamole to prevent it from browning and refrigerate.

Nutritional Information

Serving Size: 1 (40 g)

Servings Per Recipe: 12

Amount Per Serving

Calories 55 Calories from Fat 44

% Daily Value

Total Fat 5g 7%

Saturated Fat 1g 3%

Cholesterol 0mg

Sodium 51mg 2%

Total Carbohydrate 3g 1%

Dietary Fiber 2g 9%

Sugars 0g 1%

Protein 1g 1%

SPECIAL RECIPES: 08
Mexican Rice

Ingredients

- 1 tsp salt
- 1 clove garlic, minced
- 3 tbsp olive oil
- 1 cup brown rice, not instant
- 2 cup fat-free chicken broth
- 1 can (10 oz) diced tomatoes with green chilies, undrained, divided
- 1/2 cup bell pepper, chopped
- 1/2 cup onion, chopped

Directions

- Prep 10 min
- Cook 60 min
- Ready 70 min
- Heat oil. Add rice and cook until golden and toasted. Add onion, bell pepper, and garlic and lightly saute.
- Put salt, 1/2 cup tomatoes, and broth in a blender. Process until smooth.
- Slowly add liquid from the blender to the rice mixture. If you want extra tomato, drain and add the rest of them to the rice.
- Bring to a boil, cover, turn heat to low, and simmer until rice is tender, about 1 hour (or as directed on the package).
- Do not remove the lid during the cooking process.

Note: If you don't have fresh garlic, you can add 1/2 teaspoon garlic powder to the blender.

Nutritional Information

Serving Size: 1 (140 g)

Servings Per Recipe: 6

Amount Per Serving

Calories 192 Calories from Fat 70

% Daily Value

Total Fat 8g 12%

Saturated Fat 1g 5%

Cholesterol 0mg

Sodium 890mg 37%

Total Carbohydrate 28g 9%

Dietary Fiber 2g 6%

Sugars 1g 4%

Protein 4g 6%

SPECIAL RECIPES: 09
Stir Fried Chinese Vegetables

Ingredients

- 1/4 cup chicken broth
- 1 tbsp low-sodium soy sauce
- 2 garlic cloves, minced
- 1 1/2 tsp fresh ginger, peeled and minced
- 2 cup bok choy, chopped
- 1 red bell pepper, seeded and cut into 1 inch squares
- 1 cup snow peas
- 1/2 carrot, thinly sliced
- 1/4 cup canned sliced bamboo shoots, drained
- 1/4 cup canned sliced water chestnuts, drained

Directions

- Prep 5 min
- Cook 7 min
- Ready 12 min

* In a small bowl, combine chicken broth, soy sauce, garlic and ginger.
* In a large nonstick skillet or wok, heat the oil. Stir fry bok choy and bell pepper for 3 minutes; add the broth mixture, snow peas and carrot. Reduce heat and cook, stirring frequently, until the vegetables are tender-crisp and sauce thickens, about 3 minutes.
* Stir in bamboo shoots and water chestnuts; cook, stirring frequently, until heated through, about 1 minute.

Nutritional Information

Serving Size: 1 (136 g)

Servings Per Recipe: 4

Amount Per Serving

Calories 42   Calories from Fat 3

% Daily Value

Total Fat 0g

Saturated Fat 0g

Cholesterol 0mg

Sodium 212mg 8%

Total Carbohydrate 8g 2%

Dietary Fiber 2g 9%

Sugars 4g 14%

Protein 3g 5%

SPECIAL RECIPES: 10
Cauliflower Poppers

Ingredients

- 1 head cauliflower
- 1/2 tsp ground cumin
- 1/2 tsp chili powder, or to taste
- 1/2 tsp salt
- 1/2 tsp black pepper

Directions

- Prep 10 min
- Cook 10 min
- Ready 20 min
- Preheat oven to 400 degrees F (200 degrees C).
- Cut cauliflower into florets and place in a bowl.
- Add cumin, chili powder, salt and pepper and toss well to coat.
- Coat a baking sheet with cooking spray.

- Spread cauliflower on sheet and bake until tender, about 10 minutes, stirring once during baking.

Nutritional Information

Serving Size: 1 (74 g)

Servings Per Recipe: 8

Amount Per Serving

Calories 20 Calories from Fat 2

% Daily Value

Total Fat 0g

Saturated Fat 0g

Cholesterol 0mg

Sodium 170mg 7%

Total Carbohydrate 4g 1%

Dietary Fiber 2g 6%

Sugars 1g 5%

Protein 2g 2%

CONCLUSION

This looks like a good thing to know. From this ebook, you have go on to find out what is a healthy weight for you. Weight Watchers has a simple approach to losing weight. You need to learn how to control your appetite and to beat temptation. You eat filling foods so you will eat less. You learn to make smart choices. You rely on the plan; choose with your points system. Then you adapt the plan to fit your lifestyle. This isn't really a diet; it is a new approach to eating.

If you are looking for a plan with a little flexibility but still will get you the end result of healthy weight loss and a slimmer you, give Weight Watchers a try. Combining its eating regimen with any workout or regular exercise, you will see excellent results.

Finally the best thing about weight watchers is that it is not a diet plan but a lifestyle that you can stay on to maintain a healthy weight. You have to allow enough time to be successful because there are many people who quit plans to early and they do not get the benefit of reaching there weight loss goals.

Remember that losing weight takes effort on your part but when you find a plan such as weight watchers it can make it much easier for you.